THE HUMANITIES APPROACH TO THE
MODERN SECONDARY SCHOOL CURRICULUM

The Humanities Approach to the Modern Secondary School Curriculum

BERNARD S. MILLER

The Center for Applied Research in Education, Inc.
New York

Printed in the United States of America
C3499-5

To Betty

*and to our children who have
helped us learn and age gracefully—*

Steve, Don, Jeff and Cyral

ABOUT THE AUTHOR

Bernard S. Miller, Ed. D., has been actively involved with humanities education for more than a decade. First as a participant at Williams College in 1959 and then for five years as associate director of the John Hay Fellows Humanities Program, he was jointly responsible for recommending teachers to receive fellowships at six universities across the nation—Harvard, Yale, Columbia, Northwestern, Chicago, and the University of California at Berkeley. In addition, he served as director of month-long Summer Institutes in the Humanities at Bennington College, Colorado College, and the University of Oregon.

Dr. Miller has written many articles on the humanities for publications such as *The New York State Education Journal, The Virginia Journal of Education, Social Education,* and *The English Journal.* He was a U.S. representative at the international seminar on "Individuality," Ditchley Park, Oxfordshire, England, and in 1969 served as an advisor and evaluator for the New York Foreign Studies Institutes. In August 1970, he was consultant on humanistic affairs to the Swedish Ministry of Education.

An associate of Dr. James B. Conant on his study of American high schools, Dr. Miller is the author of the article "Comprehensive High Schools" in *The Encyclopedia of Education* (New York: Macmillan, 1970). His career includes service as a teacher of history and later principal at Peekskill (New York) High School. Dr. Miller is presently Director of Campus Schools and Professor of Education at Hunter College of the City University of New York.

Harmonizing
Learning and Doing

The Humanities Approach to the Modern Secondary School Curriculum answers the current cry for relevancy in education. The guidelines suggested in this book for a multidisciplinary, humanistic curriculum can help change the school's traditional "senior slump" into a senior stimulant. Students in the humanities curriculum here described were given opportunities to become producer-oriented rather than merely consumers of education.

For three years more than 250 students in four different classes, and teachers representing the disciplines of art, English, music, social studies, drama, and the dance, have worked together in the development of the program. Both student desires and student needs were the focus of the plan which finally evolved. We are confident that similar processes can be applied with comparable success in schools across the country—and without adding to the regular school budget.

A humanities curriculum is particularly appropriate for schools wishing to combine academic study with creative experiences in a variety of the disciplines. By interrelating thought and action, a humanities curriculum harmonizes education in school with the real world outside the classroom. The artificial separation between learning and doing is healed.

Even more important: a humanities curriculum enables a school to transform its present unrelated smorgasbord of courses into a unified and purposeful sequence. Traditional vested interests and the forces of inertia have decreed that all the disciplines in our schools today be taught as autonomous subjects in isolation from all the others. Civilization's total impact on man is never studied, is never even considered. As a result, students leave school with fragmented knowledge and few reference points that encompass more than a single subject. No wonder they see school as something separate from life.

This book was written for educators who recognize how arbitrary and sterile are the conventional subject-centered curricula in our schools. Loyalty to subjects as the central hinge of education is like a stout safe in which we keep the family rhinestones. The humanities curriculum described in these pages is specifically designed to embrace a multidisciplinary, integrated approach to learning.

One essential caveat. Any humanities curriculum, to be successful, must be built on the strength and the spirit of each school. It must be custom-made. Nearly every week we receive letters from school administrators or teachers, which take the following pattern:

> We are anxious to begin a humanities course in our school next term. Please send me a copy of your humanities program which we can use for our course.

Our answer is to warn against the unquestioned adoption of any pre-packaged, mass-produced, imported humanities course, whether it is given the seal of approval from Hunter or any other place. The backgrounds and interests of the students, the talents of the teachers, the location and willingness of the community to support the program, are all prime components in determining aims and content. Even the tools of the humanities curriculum— books, films, slides, disciplines, and scheduling, cannot be borrowed from one school by another without considering the local complex.

A humanities curriculum can affect the minds and hearts of students. Both teachers and students will share and learn and be touched in ways that the regular subject offerings and schedules never approach. "We have made so many new friends this year," a senior commented at a faculty-student humanities planning session, "since we've been rearranged into groups that force us to know one another as human beings rather than merely as students and teachers."

Anyone involved in the formulation of a humanities program should be acutely aware of the disparity between lofty goals and solid deeds. Clichés can be easily spouted; they can also be easily spotted. "Whatever is educationally desirable is administratively possible" is such a cliché. I used to quote this statement every September at the first faculty meeting, as a means of encouraging the staff to develop fresh ideas. Invariably, several teachers accept the challenge and they do propose new approaches to learning. In the process, they sometimes force me to adopt "an administrative hedge." Like the pigs in George Orwell's *Animal Farm,* I have found it expedient, on occasion, to change the commandments on the wall to read:

All educational improvements are desirable
But some educational improvements are more desirable
than others.

The question, of course, is a matter of determining priorities. What areas do we emphasize: Where do we allocate our funds? Why? For schools preparing young people to live in a constantly changing world, one of the highest priorities in time, energy, space and thought, we believe, should be the development of a multidisciplinary humanities curriculum. It can be an exhilarating experience for both the faculty and the students.

It can also be frightening. Grades are abolished; students are offered free time during the school day to use the community as a learning laboratory; teachers are asked to learn *with* students, to teach with colleagues from other disciplines, to deal with the explosive issues of race, religion, patriotism, sex, and morality, without any prior agreement on permissible limits. To ask this of and for a generation of students who are eager to challenge everything and to accept nothing as an eternal verity, requires considerable faith in humanity. And steady nerves.

This book offers practical assistance for educators who want to do something about the current image of school as a place that is bad for children. A humanities curriculum points in fresh directions. It makes the subject teacher crucial but no longer central to all learning. It throws the spotlight on the teacher and the student, learning together. It provides a multidisciplinary framework in which man's angelic and his bestial qualities, his possibilities and his hang-ups, can be examined and understood.

Our humanities curriculum does not follow the preachments of the "feeling" school of behavorial scientists or the technological romantics. Social engineering concepts for education made a big splash and subsequently drowned in the 1930s. A successful reincarnation in the 1970s seems doubtful. The school alone cannot change all human nature and society. Joseph Featherstone, reviewing one of the current wave of utopian educational schemes for the year 2000 and beyond, tells an interesting tale:

> ... a teacher, in the course of a long conversation, finally convinced a benevolent-looking psychiatrist that children's day-dreaming was an important part of their learning. The psychiatrist then began to insist that day-dreaming should be added to the curriculum.[1]

A successful humanities curriculum will be a balance—perhaps a compromise, between extremes. It does not assume that all the knowledge of the world must be mastered. Neither does it assume that all learning must be intuitive and unstructured. It is based on faith as well as fact, on the importance of seeing feelingly as well as pursuing knowledge. A humanistic curriculum does not substitute play for Plato or have either in the course of study if they prove meaningless to students. Nor is it a panacea. Mistakes will be made. Fundamental beliefs will be questioned in ways that may bring forth more heat than light, more rage than respect. But both students and teachers will learn, they will have fun, and they will grow in both competence and compassion.

Emerson has written, "With every influx of light comes new danger ... in nature nothing can be given, all things are sold."[2] A humanities curriculum will be purchased at great cost to the

---

[1]*New York Times Book Review,* August 24, 1969, p. 34.

[2]Ralph Waldo Emerson, "Compensation," *Essays* (Boston: Houghton Mifflin Co., 1883), p. 104.

simplicities of educational existence. I think, I know, it is a bargain.

—*Bernard S. Miller*

ACKNOWLEDGMENTS

Most people are fortunate if they have one inspiring teacher who makes a difference in their lives. I have been blessed with three. While an undergraduate at Queens College, New York City, I had as my special mentor Professor Harry Rivlin, later to become Director of Education for the entire City University of New York, and now Education Dean at Fordham University. In 1957, kind gods enabled me to become one of the four associates of Dr. James B. Conant, formerly President of Harvard University, who returned from his duties as Ambassador to the Federal Republic of Germany to conduct a nationwide study of American high schools. For more than five years in the 1960s, Dr. Charles R. Keller, the director of the John Hay Fellows Program and previously chairman of the Williams College history department, provided the kind of professional and personal friendship which is found all too seldom in colleague staff relationships. For various reasons and in various ways all three have enlarged my life.

Dr. Charles R. Keller did not create the humanities, but he is affectionately called "Mr. Humanities" because of his untiring efforts to give humanistic studies emphasis, direction and meaning. In school and college talks across the country, and in his actions, he has spoken up for the humanities. Equally significant, he has had the humanities speak up for themselves. Much of what is found in these pages as suggested humanistic paths can be traced to Dr. Keller's thinking.

Other fine people also influenced the writing of this book. To the Hunter College High School staff for their willingness to vote in favor of a humanistic school design, to Miss Mildred Busch, the assistant principal, for dealing so effectively with the necessary scheduling, to Miss Miriam Balf and her valuable contributions based on successful experiences with the school's integrated arts course, to Mrs. Jane Greenspan and Miss Miriam Burstein, whose ideas and written comments will be found in several chapters, to Miss Marie Rosso, Mrs. Rosemarie Laster, Mr. Richard Peck, Mr. Harold Carle, Mr. Rexford Slauson, Mr. Parker Baratta, Mr. Don Kaplan, Mrs. Carola Vega, Mrs. Dede Condon, Miss Alice Halpern and Mrs. Elinor Blackman for their courage and talents as teachers of the humanities curriculum at various times, I am happily indebted. And to the students! these most human youngsters who elected the humanities curriculum and then made certain that *their* ideas were reflected; to them we are particularly appreciative.

A special word of praise and thanks goes to the ladies in front of the typewriters for their patience and skill in translating the author's hieroglyphics into typewritten material. Miss Marian Kohn, formerly the executive secretary of the John Hay Fellows Program, prepared an initial draft, and Mrs. Cynthia Caloritis has labored at length with successive changes. To them, and to Miss Anne Galschjodt, my secretary at Hunter, and our faithful assistant, Miss Rosanne Grimaldi, I am deeply thankful.

Finally, a grateful bow to the National Foundation on the Arts and the Humanities for their willingness to help support out initial efforts.

Contents

CHAPTER 1

Innovating with a Humanities Curriculum–
A Basis for Action

Humanities courses are in fashion. Titles such as "How I Teach the Humanities" and "Relevance and Articulation with the Humanities" will be found in national English, social studies, and fine arts journals as well as in more generalized teacher and administrative bulletins. Indeed, programs in the humanities have become so popular that several school and college people have begun to attack humanities courses in these same journals. An extensive bibliography of heavy and lightweight books on the humanities is now available. In 1969, a national association for humanities teachers was organized which issues a quarterly journal dealing primarily with humanities programs.[1] The Catholic University of America Curriculum Development Center in Washington, D.C., has a special issue on humanities courses in ten elementary and secondary schools.[2] An annotated list of more than 200

---

[1] Herbert Safran, editor, *The Humanities Journal,* National Association For Humanities Education (Shanendehowa Central School, Elnora, New York, 12065).

[2] Sister Dolores Brady, editor, *Curriculum Information Services* (Washington, D.C. 20017: Catholic University of America, March, 1971) Volume II, Number 5.

humanities courses across the United States has been compiled by the National Council of Teachers of English.[3] Actually, when this number is compared with the more than 25,000 high schools, the swing to the humanities is, in reality, far from an established pattern. But movement toward the humanities in our schools is discernible. In this sense, humanities courses are now the "in thing."

Happily, for once, what is educationally stylish is both possible and desirable. As we shall see, it takes no magic wand to move the traditional separate courses in social studies and English into a humanistic program of studies. In virtually every school in the United States, English and social studies are required subjects for all students. Without running to the local board of education, a school staff could reorganize its schedule of subjects to bring these mandated courses into a closer and more meaningful harmony. Art, music, and the other humanistic disciplines will involve more extensive efforts if they are to be integrated with English and social studies.

But the question and procedure of changing to a humanities program necessitate far more than a simple shuffling of courses. Too much of education has been altered superficially on a piecemeal basis. Someone has referred to this technique as the application of Band-Aids to internal bleeding. Education seems to grow most successfully in its terminology.

If we wish to have more than a pretense of educational progress, the development of a viable humanities curriculum will require many sessions with the entire humanities faculty as well as with the parents and students. Nor will the humanities curriculum ever be "finished." As we shall see, the beauty of the humanities lies precisely in its continuous growth and reinterpretations as new events, new participants, and new resources and materials occasion fresh discoveries. In this sense, the humanities curriculum is always evolving, always new and stimulating.

DEFINING THE HUMANITIES

What do we mean when we say that we teach the humanities?

---

[3]Richard R. Adler and Arthur Applebee, eds., *Annotated Humanities Programs,* National Council of Teachers of English (Champaign, Ill., 61820: Spring, 1968).

The dictionary definition will not do. Here, for example, is the statement in *Webster's New World Dictionary:*

> the humanities, 1. language and literature, especially the classical Greek and Latin 2. the branches of learning concerned with human thought and relations, as distinguished from the sciences; especially literature and philosophy, and often the fine arts, history, etc.[4]

Missing from such a definition is the feeling that man is actively involved in the process of understanding and changing himself and the world about him. Missing is an indication of man's concern for and identification with humanity; missing, too, is concern for man's emotional development, his intellectual growth, and his moral, religious, and aesthetic values and drives. By studying the humanities we should gain reference points on which to make judgments. Like the earth to Antaeus, the humanities provides the strength necessary to cope with the contemporary scene. It offers meaning to existence; it offers alternatives in thought and action. Viewed in this light, the humanities becomes that cluster of attitudes, behavior patterns, and ideas which affirm our participation in mankind.

THE SEGMENTED CURRICULUM

Courses in the humanistic disciplines—art, music, literature, history, foreign language, dance and drama—have always been offered by schools. Unfortunately, these subjects are considered as separate and unequal parts. Never are they interrelated; never are they studied beyond the limitations imposed by a single discipline; never is the school curriculum examined as a totality. Artificially separating the entire school day by subjects has resulted in a neat scheduling pattern. But the compartmentalization of subjects has imposed rigid restraints which have left students with no sense of unity or personal relationship to the school curriculum, and to life outside the school.

---

[4]Joseph H. Friend and David B. Guralnik, editors, *Webster's New World Dictionary* (New York: The World Publishing Company, 1958), p. 707.

Follow a typical high school student from class to class in a single day and the absurdity of the present arrangement becomes painfully clear. Each time the bell rings the student moves Pavlov-fashion from one subject to another, from English to social studies to physical education, science, mathematics and foreign language courses. Nearly always there is a pause for lunch, a home room session, perhaps a study hall period, and possibly another elective. In each class the teacher neither is aware nor really cares what the students in her room are taught in the other classes. Each course is studied in isolation—in isolation from other subjects and often in isolation from the same subject taught in previous years.

American history, for example, in many states is a required course in grades five, eight and eleven. Undergraduate students are fated to be enrolled for still a fourth time in a college-level American history course. An examination of each syllabus will show that in successive grades the battles, the presidents and the great issues are generally covered in greater detail, and different texts are used. But memories do not willingly retain what Alfred North Whitehead has called "inert ideas—ideas that are merely received into the mind without being utilized, or tested, or thrown into fresh combinations."[5] Instead of building on what has been learned before, students are forced to repeat the process.

Why? A major factor in students' almost instant memory loss after completing a social studies course is their lack of identification with the material to be mastered. Each year, as students move from one grade level to the next, they are forced to hear the same long-playing record from the front of the room:

> How could you be so stupid? Didn't the teacher last year cover
> this material on the presidents of the United States?

In the past, the students were too polite, or too cowed, or too wise to reply. But if the teacher could have read what the eyes reflected, he might have learned the answer:

> Yes, dear social studies teacher, we had the presidents of the
> United States last year. We had to learn the presidents, and some
> years even the vice-presidents, in grades three and five and seven
> and eight and again in our junior or senior year. But to us they

---

[5] Alfred North Whitehead, *The Aims of Education* (New York: The Free Press, 1967), p. 1.

are only names, only skeletons, only dead people in textbooks. Why can't you bring them alive in the classroom, make us interested in them as human beings who loved and hated, laughed and felt pain, who expressed doubts as well as beliefs? Perhaps so many of us are refusing to look back, or we look back in anger, because we sense nothing dynamic, nothing relevant in the past as you teach it to our world of today.

For most students, history and the social studies provide too narrow, too still a compass.

By examining life through the prism of a single discipline in isolation from the others, we give students a disjointed view of civilization. Little wonder that students find the segmented curriculum to be alien to their lives. Never are they given an opportunity to puncture some holes in the walls that have separated each of the disciplines; never are they shown or allowed to discover for themselves the continuity of life as it is reflected in art, music, history, literature, drama, philosophy, and the dance. Spirit and variety in man's expressions are removed. Instead the students are fed the separate parts.

Unlike mathematics, in the humanities the sum can be greater than the separate parts. And students do enjoy the fresh perspectives they encounter when the disciplines are interreleated. Consider how learning could be reinforced and enriched if, when discussing the world-wide depression of the 1930s, the English teacher, the social studies teacher, the foreign language teacher, and the teachers of music and art coordinate their disciplines. Students could then feel the reverberations of the event on every aspect of man's experience. But our schools have packaged all knowledge into artificial cubicles. Instead of viewing school learning and school life as a totality, we offer a jigsaw puzzle of odds and ends and simply assume that the students will make the necessary connections. Most students do not. In "What Fifty Said" Robert Frost could have been describing the present school curriculum when he wrote, "I gave up fire for form till I was cold."[6]

---

[6]From "What Fifty Said" from *The Poetry of Robert Frost* edited by Edward Connery Lathem. Copyright 1928 by Holt, Rinehart and Winston, Inc. Copyright © 1956 by Robert Frost. Reprinted by permission of Holt, Rinehart and Winston, Inc.

We wonder about the infinite capacity of the student's mind to resist the intrusion of knowledge. But if knowledge does not hang together, the students see no necessity to pay attention.

WHAT STUDENTS WANT

Actually even the movement toward an integration of the disciplines into a humanities curriculum is only a partial step in the needed radical restructuring of our schools. Competition as a healthy concomitant of school life is no longer accepted by many young people as an inherent good. They are more in tune with the spirit of sharing, with the concept of cooperation rather than competition. They rebel against an overstructured society and an overstructured school. Respect for authority, age, and custom has no great credence for the generations born in the aftermath of the atomic bomb. The traditional stress on the verbal and numerical notion of human measurement and worth is out of tune with many of today's student attitudes and aims. To be creative is for them more important than to be scholarly. They wish to be freed rather than bound by their learning.

Other students see the meaning of life in a different light. To experience everything new, to live for the moment, is more realistic for an increasing number of students than to save for a rainy day. Television commercials promoting everything from bank loans to beer reinforce their desire to "live it up" in the here and now, because tomorrow may never come. Such students find it difficult to swallow a 12 or 13 year school program of daily traditional work and study leading to eventual graduation and future rewards at age 17 or 18.

Students will differ on their priorities, on wanting more possessions or more power, but they all agree on wanting more, and wanting it now. They wish to share in the determination of the forces that are shaping their lives. They insist that the process of educational and emotional growth and development is too important to be left to adults. They have taken seriously our statements about democracy. They want to participate. And their study of history convinces them that young people cannot make many worse mistakes than those made by their parents. The clamor to lower the voting age to 18 is one sign of this attitude. Taking an active role in deciding on curriculum requirements, course content and grades is another. With good reason, students resent being considered merely as a number in a teacher's roll book rather than as a human being. At a community open school night, a teacher asked the parents to sit in the seats occupied during the day by their children. "Otherwise," she confessed, "I will not be able to identify your child. I make it a policy not to know the child's name so I am not influenced by the personality of the child when I give him a grade." Unfortunately, in too many schools children are known by the seats they occupy and not as individuals.

Certainly our schools and colleges have a healthy situation when students feel that they are actively involved in the process of learning. A humanities curriculum can change the last year of high school from a senior slump to a senior stimulant when students are considered and consulted. But more is necessary than just the formalities of participation.

Students must *feel* that they are contributing significantly in developing and directing *their* program. Indeed, nearly any new course of study that is cooperatively designed, that is imaginative, and is not overly weighted with tedious moralizing, will prove attractive to students. A humanities program will succeed when the appeal is visceral as well as cerebral, when the crucial issues asked by young people throughout time are faced—identity, kinship, value, the search for a meaningful life.

What students want is to integrate learning around moral ends and to internalize rather than just intellectualize, to feel and taste what has to be learned. What students want is not necessarily what students need. But the characteristic style of most of our schools seems to be preparing young people for a world long dead. In this looking backward approach to education, the schools serve merely as echoes of a society that once was rather than as harbingers of the future.

Even the most radical students will agree that the fundamental and technical skills to be mastered in an increasingly complex society must be stressed. But the commitment to utilize these skills in a humane and intelligent manner must receive equal stress in our schools. At present we are pouring in more and more material for students to memorize without allowing them time to think, to digest, to interpret.

The following story is told about Harold Pinter after he agreed to write a special one-hour television play. When the play was read aloud for the first time, everyone agreed that the script was excellent. But when the producer asked for the time score, he was informed that the scheduled one-hour drama lasted exactly twenty-eight minutes and thirty-four seconds. An awkward silence followed. Then Mr. Pinter looked about and said, "You see, there are quite a lot of full pauses . . . "[7]

In school, we abhor a pause, whether full or empty. It is almost as though we are certain the students will get into some mischief if we give them time to wonder, time to think. I fear that too many Boards of Education and school administrators react the same way about free time for teachers. And so we move along much too rapidly, much too perfunctorily, and like an iceberg, reveal far too little of the whole. The ripples of meaning, the reverberations from full pauses are drowned. Needed desperately is a radical shifting in the structure, style, and emphasis of our schools from the pursuit of knowledge as an end in itself to a moral imperative. A humanities curriculum can be designed with these goals in mind.

In a real sense, a revolution has already taken place in the attitude of our students. In the 1950s most students either resisted or were passive about the education handed to them. Today they ask, more, they demand that education mean something other than time spent and credits received. And if the educators cannot or will not hear their cry for moral meaning, they are prepared, sometimes confidently, sometimes arrogantly, to point the way themselves.

Students today wish to define school goals not in terms of academic courses but in areas of concern, in developing sensitivity for others, an aesthetic sense, and a deepening power to examine and think critically and creatively. What a man is, for many young people, has become more important than what a man does. Provide students an opening to help explore such concerns in conjunction with the faculty and going to school will erase the false dichotomy between work and play.

---

[7] *The New York Times,* July 13, 1969, Sec. 4, p. 8.

THE PREPARATION OF TEACHERS

For such a changed classroom atmosphere and for such a student-teacher relationship to prevail, the present program of teacher preparation and orientation will also have to be radically overhauled. Consciously or unconsciously, as teachers and school administrators, we have allowed ourselves to become, and allowed the educational system to make us, predictable. We are more addicted to regularity than variety. Author James Hilton diagnosed the disease with surgeon-like precision in his famous character Mr. Chips:

> He had begun to sink into that creeping rot of pedagogy which is the worst and ultimate pitfall of the profession; giving the same lesson year after year, he had found a groove into which the other affairs of his life adjusted themselves with insidious ease. He worked well, he was conscientious; he was a fixture that gave service, satisfaction, confidence, everything except inspiration.[8]

Chips changed when he met another human being who helped him gain a wider vision concerning the possibilities of his students and his subject. Most young people who become teachers are not so fortunate. They learn to imitate the traditional teaching models before them. Unfortunately, the vast majority of educational institutions are filled with college professors and school teachers who are immune to the new directions and the new designs of the arts, the mass media, and human relations in classroom teaching. For the most part educators follow the standard operating procedures of a medieval university. They lecture. It has been observed that the lecture method of teaching provides the easiest way to get information from the teacher's notebook to the student's notebook without affecting the student's mind.

"Publish or perish," that much abused cliché, is still the main road to success in the world of academe. To be a dynamic teacher is no crime, but it pays far fewer dividends in prestige and promotion than scholarly studies. No real incentives are offered the educational fraternity to stimulate students to think for themselves, to ask the right questions, to exchange ideas. Our teachers of teachers, the education professors, are as guilty as their

---

[8]James Hilton, *Good-bye, Mr. Chips* (Boston: Little, Brown, and Co., 1962), p. 36.

distant cousins in the established disciplines in downgrading classroom participation. As a result, teaching has become the dreary routine one muddles through in order to treasure the true rewards of being a professor—the chance to write, to work with a small group of graduate students in your own narrow area of interest, and to engage in lucrative out-of-college research programs. Too few college professors take time to really know their students, to understand their backgrounds, their needs, their hopes. Instead, the emphasis is on material to be mastered, or at least covered. Assignments become an end in themselves. They are mimeographed, distributed, and collected. The human element is rarely noticed. The explanations, the excuses for this sad state of educational affairs are legion. But for students it all adds up to the same result—an education that is impersonal, indifferent, and irrelevant.

Here, then, is the ultimate question we must face if education is to be redesigned into a humanistic framework. It makes little sense for a community, a board of education, or a school administrator to revolutionize the school and move from a subject-centered to a humanities-centered curriculum if the practitioners, the teachers, are fundamentally insensitive to the desires and uniqueness of each student. A humanities program will succeed in direct ratio to the humaneness of the faculty.

THE IMPORTANCE OF THE FACULTY

No matter how well meaning a faculty, no matter how well motivated a student body and school community to a humanities curriculum, the inadvisability of *forcing* teachers from different disciplines to work together cannot be overstated. Some teachers are constitutionally unable to share the blackboard with colleagues. Often they are dynamic individuals with personalities so strong that they find subordinating their ideas to those of a fellow teacher to be an impossible assignment. These people function best when functioning alone with students. Lecturing is their primary tool.

Sometimes a teacher is too shy, too irritable, or too opinionated to welcome colleague contact every day with the same students. Sometimes we have adults in the classroom who should have been removed from both students and teachers a long time ago. Such teachers banked their educational fires as soon as they received tenure. And their tenure status holds them in the system like wet salt in a shaker—no matter how much banging and knocking, nothing pours out. Sometimes a teacher is not sufficiently confident of her ability in front of colleagues because she lacks teaching experience. Actually, no better program to gain confidence and experience can be devised by a school system than to team a new with a seasoned teacher.

The unanswered question is not just confidence or experience, but whether the teachers are compatible, whether they are in general agreement on the goals of the course and the best ways to work with students. What is considered acceptable practice for one teaching team can be poison for another. A textbook author has a prize letter from a teacher who wrote, "Please take question two on page 97 out of your next edition. Every time we get to it, it only leads to a discussion."

Never underestimate the crucial importance of the faculty in developing a humanities program—or anything else. Far more humanities courses have floundered and failed because the teachers on the team were mismatched than from an inadequate curriculum. More than in traditional subjects, a humanities teacher must be willing to expose her ignorance in front of colleagues as well as in front of students, must be prepared to listen as well as suggest, must be considerate of adult idiosyncrasies. The humanities teacher must also be ready to spend additional hours learning about the contemporary world of students outside the school. The new moods in music, art, dance, drama, sex, architecture, and religion are often loud, unfamiliar, uncomfortable, and frightening. In short, teachers for a humanities program simply cannot be selected and replaced like interchangeable parts of an automobile. They must come to the program custom-made. Administrators who dump mediocre teachers into a humanities program in the hope that a metamorphosis will take place merely delude themselves. If we wish to help our students become more human, we must have a great deal of humanity in ourselves.

A high intelligence quotient is not the most important attribute required in an excellent teacher for the humanities. First is character—a feeling for people, a sense of compassion, moral integrity, and faith. Second is effectiveness—an ability to understand and be understood. Intelligence comes third in the trinity of essential traits. Without character and the ability to communicate as coordinate allies, intelligence will prove to be an inadequate teacher resource. Of course we can all point to striking exceptions. A teacher may be so gifted intellectually that students in the room are constantly challenged by the daily explosions of knowledge. Most often, the knowledge fails to register because the students are turned off.

THE HUMANITIES AND THE SCIENCES

Although the humanities encompasses all ideas which affirm our participation in mankind, few attempts have been made by schools to deal directly with mathematics and science in a humanities curriculum. The sciences and the humanities are not in conflict. But the collaboration problems for the humanistic disciplines alone are so complex that the science specializations have been sidetracked.

Prejudice on the part of those who subscribe to Lord Snow's two-culture thesis[9] is also evident in the decision to exclude science from the humanities curriculum. "The sciences teach us how to wind the clock; the humanities warn us what time it is" illustrates such bias. So too are comments insisting that the humanities is primarily concerned with the "why," with the personal, the subjective, the emotional, the spiritual, and the moral. The sciences, so goes the argument, simply concentrate on the "how" of life.

Actually the humanities and the sciences are complementary. Both provide options for what we can do and what we should do. The totality of living is not separated artificially into a twin-headed being, one called science and the other humanities. René Dubos has observed that while man is the product of his social and cultural history, "everything he does is conditioned by his biological attributes. The performance of each human group reflects biological necessities and propensities inherited from the evolutionary and experimental past."[10]

---

[9]Charles P. Snow, *Two Cultures and A Second Look* (New York: Cambridge University Press, 1969).

[10]René Dubos, "Humanistic Biology," in *The American Scientist* (Berkeley, California, 1965), No. 53.

Unless those of us who proclaim the humanities are also scientifically literate, we cannot deal with modern technology and make rational judgments about the race to outer space, ecology, and atomic power plants. Science need not be taught as a politically neutral subject without social values. And the humanities must not be taught as though it was impervious to our scientific world. Both disciplines need association if we are to develop a viable learning environment with benchmarks for reflection and action. Bridges between these two areas require immediate building.

Actually, neither of the disciplines can be said to be definitive. Neither discipline needs to suffer the fallacy of dogmatic finality. Answers accepted today to the problems of living a meaningful life may be completely wrong for another individual, and at another time. If the sciences give options on what we can do, the humanities provides alternatives based on values. Although the totality of living is not separated artificially into a twin-headed being, one called science and the other humanities, the actual structure of the disciplines, and their benchmarks for reflection and action have made such divisions an acceptable learning procedure in the past. We need fresh thinking for the present and the future.

Unfortunately, the two cultures are not treated as equals in school or society. The National Science Foundation was funded by our federal government for more than a decade before consideration was given to the establishment of a National Foundation on the Arts and the Humanities. Congress regularly appropriates 500 millions and more for the National Science Foundation; the eleemosynary brothers in the National Foundation on the Arts and the Humanities are budgeted for less than 50 millions.

We do live in a scientific rather than a humanistic age. Money and emphasis are allocated in accordance with what Congress and the President consider our national need and our national purpose. The first federal funds to retrain teachers following the Soviet Sputnik success in 1957 were earmarked for teachers of mathematics, the sciences, and foreign languages. By labeling the bill the National Education Defense Act, Congress was willing to approve this special legislation to support special interests.

A study conducted by the Educational Testing Service of Princeton, New Jersey, in 1969 covering 38,000 students from more than 7,500 academic high schools taking the College Entrance Board achievement test revealed what most school people already knew:

> Changes in the teaching of mathematics and science are now common to many schools. The teaching of history and social studies has remained substantially the same in the last ten years. Only moderate changes have occurred in the English curriculum.[11]

Hopefully sometime before the year 2000 A.D., some schools and colleges will have initiated a total curriculum in which all the disciplines will be related and integrated. At the moment the two cultures remain far from the academic marriage bed. By no means does this mean that science and science teachers should be excluded from a humanities program. The discipline of science is most pertinent in any humanistic discussion—analysis of the race question, and the question of air and water pollution are but two examples. Similarly, a mathematics teacher can make a significant contribution when a humanities program is dealing with the consequences of a computerized society. Science and mathematics can be interpreted and studied as humanistic disciplines. Knowledge of facts does make values significant. But the blending of the two cultures into a single coordinated curriculum has still not reached the courtship stage. When most people refer to the humanistic subjects in our schools and colleges today, mathematics and science are unfortunately excluded. Virtually all the other disciplines—English, history, the social sciences, the fine and related arts, philosophy, music, foreign language study, architecture, drama, and the dance—are considered to be members of the humanistic fraternity.

ORGANIZING A HUMANITIES PROGRAM

When a school faculty does decide to offer a humanities program, what procedure is recommended? The most common

---

[11]Elizabeth W. Haven, "A Survey of the Academic Preparation of College Board Candidates," *Educational Testing Service* (Princeton, New Jersey 08540; 1969).

pattern of humanities organization is to have the disciplines of English and social studies coordinated. Sometimes one of these two disciplines serves as a fulcrum for one or more of the other subjects—music, art, drama, philosophy, and the dance. Occasionally one hears of a humanities course limited to the fine arts. Courses and teachers frequently are combined, either formally for a single or double period of English and social studies, or informally when, for example, a social studies teacher invites an art teacher to describe the artistic style of an era.

Having two or more teachers coordinate a multidisciplinary approach to learning generates a new dimension to the school curriculum. That so few schools have seen fit to provide such cross fertilization of ideas is a commentary on the power of inertia as well as of vested interests.

Once a school agrees to initiate a humanities program, flexible scheduling becomes the name of the game. Fortunately, neither the formulation of new goals nor the rescheduling of classes need cost an additional penny. Assume, for example, an average of 25 to 30 students in English and social studies classes. By scheduling the English and social studies teachers to meet the same students consecutively, the school system could set the stage for the organization of a humanities program without any additional expenditures. Here is a typical program for these students and teachers:

Period I —English teacher with 25 students
—history teacher with 30 students

Period II —English teacher with 30 students
—history teacher with 25 students

Time for the two teachers to meet and plan the joint course of study must be provided. In schools where the teachers are assigned five teaching periods each day plus a study hall and an official class (homeroom) as the normal class load, judicious scheduling can again keep the budget in balance. For example, the administrator could assign other teachers to handle the official class or study hall thereby freeing the English and social studies teachers for a daily conference. Or study halls could be combined—better still, eliminated, and the students reassigned to more meaningful classes. In schools where contractual agreements prevent swapping of classes or special considerations given to certain teachers, students could meet fewer than five consecutive days each week in humanities classes. Offering students independent study opportunities away from teachers during the school day makes excellent educational sense. It also provides time for the teaching team to meet. Sometimes when no free time via flexible scheduling can be arranged, teachers have found or made time during lunch or after school to assure the needed coordination of the disciplines in a humanities program.

Even where the administration is uncooperative or unimaginative, teachers can initiate a multidisciplinary humanities program. An English and a social studies teacher meeting with the same students in two separate periods or with different students during the same period can exchange classes and/or dovetail their courses of study so as to highlight and integrate the two disciplines. Selection of books, themes, projects, and trips could all be coordinated. The myth that curriculum reform is entirely dependent on administrative leadership is simply not true. Virtually all the "revolutions" in the mathematics, science, and foreign language curricula were triggered by college professors, working with school teachers and supported by private foundations or federal funds. School administration in many urban and suburban localities is now too complex, and too time-consuming for the administrator to assume major initiatives in curriculum change. The daily school life pressures, the requests and demands from parents, the growing militancy of teachers and students, the preparation of endless reports, the constant struggle to locate additional space in overcrowded facilities, the problems of drugs, thieves, and willful property destruction have pushed administrative responsibility for curricula change on others. Administrators can and should provide a school climate in which new ideas will be welcomed. But effecting the kind of curriculum reform that is more than mere academic window dressing is dependent in large measure on the educational practitioners—the teachers.

ADVANTAGES OF MULTIDISCIPLINARY TEACHING TEAMS

For both students and teachers, the back-to-back double period arrangement means tremendous scheduling flexibility. No longer does the learning in each classroom have to be terminated arbitrarily at the conclusion of a 45 or 50 minute period. A film can be seen and discussed on the same day. A guest speaker can address both classes at the same time. A panel discussion can involve more students than a single class.

Other opportunities are evident. With a teaching team one teacher could meet with both classes for the two periods while the second teacher meets individual students for a double period. The teachers could then exchange programs for a double period on the succeeding day. All the students could meet in a large session with both teachers for part of a period and then reorganize into small student-led discussion groups for the remainder of the time. A trip to a nearby museum can be arranged with no disturbance to the rest of the school and without removing the students from other classes. The English and history teachers could even meet each class separately in the traditional pattern of a single period.

Varieties of Scheduling Possible
With Humanities Teaching Team in Double Period Arrangement

1.   English Teacher   Social Studies Teacher
     Per. 1   Per. 1—5 students
          $>$50 students
     Per. 2   Per. 2—5 students

2.   English and Social Studies Teachers (or Guest Speaker, Film, Trip, etc.)
     Per. 1
          $>$55 students in large group session
     Per. 2

3.   Social Studies Teacher   English Teacher
     Per. 1   Per. 1—5 students
          $>$50 students
     Per. 2   Per. 2—5 students

4.   English and Social Studies Teachers
     Per. 1—55 students for first 15 minutes
     Per. 2—student-led small discussion groups

5.   English Teacher   Social Studies Teacher
     Per. 1—25 students   Per. 1—30 students
     Per. 2—30 students   Per. 2—25 students

6.   English and Social Studies Teachers hold joint conference while students are on independent study.

Flexible scheduling via teaching teams has psychological advantages as well. A good teacher becomes an even better teacher when what he is doing with students is witnessed by a colleague. The thought processes become more acute, the questions are phrased with more precision, the knowledge that we should argue less and listen more somehow is more easily remembered. When both the English and the history teacher participate in a discussion and by chance, or by design, take opposing sides, the excitement and stimulation for the students is immeasurably increased. And if the students are encouraged to add their own contradictory ideas, the end of the session will be greeted with groans.

When two teachers in different disciplines share the decision on what to include and what to exclude, material that each never questioned before suddenly faces a fresh examination. "Why bother memorizing the correct chronological order of all the English kings," asks the English teacher, "when we might better spend the time discussing the nature of power?" "Must we read all the interminable chapters in Cervantes' *Don Quixote*," counters the social studies teacher, "when the meat of his style can be learned in the first one hundred pages?" A social studies teacher, emerging from a seminar session in which the students compared Camus' *The Plague* with Homer's *The Iliad* confessed that he was exhilarated. "When I get out of my discipline I become less concerned about coverage. I am more willing to get at the heart of things and even get off the topic if something more stimulating is on the floor for discussion." A student in this humanities program has observed, "For the first time I'm in a class where the teacher does not have all the answers." And then she added, "and neither have I."

Most important is what happens to the curriculum when teachers from different disciplines have the desire and the time to coordinate their talents. Learning takes on a new dimension when an art teacher, for example, shows Leonardo da Vinci's painting *Mona Lisa* in conjunction with the English teacher's discussion of Walter Pater's poem describing the *Mona Lisa*. Of course the English teacher could show the slide herself. But a new voice, a new thought, a different perspective to what is studied provides students with new insights for learning.

Interestingly the film media have combined music, art, and drama as well as visual history and literature with motion picture technology, to create emotional and mind-shaking experiences. The better television producers and directors have followed a similar formula. But learning in school remains almost exclusively a single subject hammering on the mind rather than appealing to the senses in an integrated structure.

Combining several teachers from different disciplines in a humanities curriculum can help refocus the subjects into the equivalent of the cinema verité. Certainly it will provide these teachers with fresh incentives to consider learning in unorthodox ways. After a number of years of teaching the same subject to the same grades even the best teachers find school work becoming a routine, a chore. Educational mold begins to form whenever new opportunities are no longer presented to recharge intellectual batteries. Yes, some teachers are self-generators and seem able to renew themselves. Most of us are not so well endowed. By deliberately placing teachers from different disciplines together, a new relationship, a new idea, a new awareness of possibilities is structured. For the teacher, the opportunity to move in novel directions is like buying a new hat, or being complimented for looking so alive.

THE CORE CURRICULUM VERSUS THE HUMANITIES

Interlacing several disciplines in a humanities program should not be confused with the core curriculum. The core curriculum organizes two or more subjects around a number of central themes. In developing the theme of conservation, for example, the core teacher uses selected literary works, poems, stories, and drama as well as historical events and even related music and painting. But a single teacher is in charge of the entire class. Unfortunately, the age of specialization has made few under-graduate or graduate education majors into renaissance figures. The strengths and weaknesses of the core teacher's background determine the depth or shallowness in the way a theme is treated. Thus an English teacher in a core curriculum will generally devote more time to literature, her special area of competence. Con-sciously or unconsciously, she will tend to shortchange the allied disciplines. In many instances the core curriculum places a low priority on the learning of knowledge. Instead the act of doing something becomes the sign of student success. Foreign language study and the rigors of higher mathematics, science, history, and literary work decline in schools where the core curriculum dominates. Nor does the core curriculum provide for a consistent flow of themes or the development of skills from one year to the next.

The experience of teachers with the core curriculum is reminiscent of the comic strip in which the restaurant-keeper advertises a 50-50 horse and rabbit stew. His customer complains that the stew has no taste of rabbit. "How did you make this 50-50 horse and rabbit stew?" he demands. "Simple," replies the cook, "I use half a rabbit and half a horse."

Most of the thrust for the core curriculum was blunted by the success of the Russian cosmonauts in the late 1950s and the subsequent stress in the United States on separate subject mastery. Today few secondary schools have a curriculum based on the core concept. Unlike the core program, the humanities curriculum enables teachers from different disciplines to pool their special resources and develop cooperatively a multidisciplinary learning environment. The difference in the two approaches is fundamental. A humanities curriculum is structured to capitalize on the unique strengths and contributions of each subject and each teacher. A sequential design is established, students are directly involved, and provision is made for creative experiences away from the textbook and the school in the humanities curriculum.

Little danger exists that the humanities program here suggested to replace the core curriculum and the learning of segregated subjects will become a "Mickey Mouse" grab bag. Every subject teacher in the humanities curriculum will guarantee that the integrity of her discipline is not debased. And within the new humanities framework, the interrelationships of subjects with other life experiences will be enhanced. As we shall see, the more disciplines involved, the better the opportunities for flexibility and stimulation.

CHAPTER 2

Deciding from the Varieties
of Humanities Programs

Humanities programs come in all shapes and sizes. Always, where successful, they emphasize values and offer students special opportunities to gain a sense of understanding about themselves, their past and their present. They deal with the feel of the fact rather than just the fact. They ask more questions than are answered—"Who am I? What is the meaning of life? Where have I come from? Where am I going? In what do I believe? Why?" Hopefully the students leave the program with an affirmation and commitment to be contributing members of the human race. A well-oriented humanities staff seeks to have the students become inner-directed, to develop a personal gyroscope on which to make judgments and to take action. In devising the program, the nature of the work determines the organizational pattern and not the other way around. Nor is the structure based primarily on administrative convenience or tradition.

Beyond this basic framework, humanities courses fly in all different directions. You will find them in elementary schools, but most frequently on the secondary level. You will find them in urban ghetto schools for students who cannot stomach reading and in wealthy suburban communities where the course may be exclusively for the intellectually elite. Some meet during the school day, some in the late afternoon, and still others are weekly evening sessions. Humanities courses are offered both for credit and on a no credit basis, with and without grades, and as an elective program limited to students specially approved by the teacher. You can find one kind of humanities course for the vocationally oriented, another for the college bound. Some schools open the course to everyone regardless of background; some schools require all students to be enrolled. In a few schools they are utilizing the mass media in general and films in particular as the principal medium whereby students express and react to ideas. Some teachers focus solely on the performance aspect of the humanities. In drama, dance, music, art, film, sculpting, pottery, and the other expressive arts, the students are offered opportunities to create their own thoughts. In mediocre programs they merely copy the thoughts of others, a type of painting by the numbers. Several teachers of the humanities emphasize an intensive study of what artists have written or shown of their inner selves. Seldom will we find a textbook anthology approach to the humanities. Paperbacks continue to serve as the most potent weapon in the armory of humanistic tools.

Most recently the commercial world has found money in selling the humanities to the schools in a package plan. "Our all-inclusive humanities course touches all bases, and covers every humanistic discipline. Religion, literature, architecture, mythology, music, philosophy, art, sculpture, and lots more are included. We discover the world of tomorrow in the life of yesterday," advertises one of the business concerns. Classes are supplied with monthly issues of a specially prepared magazine, as well as slides, films, art reproductions and other multimedia materials in what appears to be a "teacher-proof" program. Even if the teacher is totally inept, the advertisements seem to imply, once the pre-packaged humanities is shown to students, instant learning will take place. In schools where teachers have no competence to make their own selections of topics to discuss, such external programs in the humanities may be better than no program at all. But the essence of the humanities is the cross-fertilization of ideas and creative impulses when students react with students and with teachers.

Unfortunately, the overwhelming majority of business corporations provide pre-digested humanities kits which serve as courses in appreciation or cognition rather than as springboards to fresh insights. Instructional technology cannot build humaneness, sensitive interaction, and individual creative impulses into a mass-produced humanities hardware. They offer answers instead of raising questions. And the affective responses are seldom developed. In short, the packaged programs do all the thinking for both the teacher and the students.

Commercial programs can offer excellent supplemental audio-visual aids for a humanities course. The *best* audio-visual aid is the competent, compassionate teacher in the classroom. Finding and holding on to such a teacher will produce more lasting results than any humanities-of-the-month panaceas.

Chronological and thematic are the two most popular patterns of organization for humanities programs. The thematic approach is more novel for students. (They are accustomed to the chronological march or stumble over the successive civilizations of man year after year in history courses.) But a danger always exists that the disciplines may be tied together artificially in a thematic design. Not everything that relates to the architecture or literature of a specific theme, for example, may have a legitimate echo with history, music, or the other arts. Selecting the most appropriate themes to stress is another constant problem. And examining a work from a thematic base often forces the class to neglect the integrity of the work itself.

Here is one brief description of a thematic design:

> We begin with a unit on the meaning of civilization and culture and those modern scientific disciplines, archaeology and anthropology, which deal with them. Then a unit on mythology and the great religions, where the emphasis is always on a pride in one's faith and an abiding respect for the other person's way of life. Next a unit on philosophy and ethics. During the philosophy unit the students listen to Edward R. Murrow's record *This I Believe* and then write their own credos. We use the two ethical concepts of loyalty and justice since so many students now seem to be concerned with these ideas. To illustrate that what seems to be justice is not always justice, we show and discuss three films, *Les Miserables, Boomerang,* and *The Oxbow Incident.* We read what Plato, Judge Learned Hand, John Marshall, and John Milton had to say about justice. Then the students write a paper on their concept of justice now that their smug preconceptions have been challenged.

THE OVERSTUFFED HUMANITIES COURSE

Critics will be quick to comment that "to do" civilization, culture, ethics and justice in a single semester is to move at a breakneck pace and to merely gloss over some high points. Thus the curse of coverage, so common to the traditional curriculum, will once again take priority over penetration and understanding in the type of humanities program outlined above. The critics are correct. School teachers are acutely vulnerable to the disease called "the overstuffed curriculum." Somehow we have had the belief implanted that if our students do not learn everything in our class, they will never gain the knowledge in another class. And so we pour it on, "it" being whatever subject has to be covered. We need to learn a lesson from those who practice rather than teach the humanities on how to give students time to absorb and channel what has been learned rather than to overwhelm them with an endless array of "can you top this?" material.

Some humanities courses avoid an overstuffed curriculum by concentrating on specific time periods and/or specific locations—5th century Athens, 15th century Florence, and 20th century New York, for example. Other programs provide a geographical orientation and examine the culture of selected regions of the world. Still others are formalistic and deal with principles of design, harmony, and rhythm as seen in arts and crafts. Humanities courses have also been structured around great events, great men, great works, religions, philosophy, and a combination of such patterns.

Again, whatever the organization, the focus should be on humanity's successful and unsuccessful efforts to understand and deal with a world in motion. The exact format should be predicated on what students have already experienced in previous courses and in their lives, and on the strengths and interests of the faculty.

REPRESENTATIVE HUMANITIES COURSES

One of the healthy problems faced in listing specific humanities courses in schools across the country is that the courses will not stay put. The best courses are constantly reorganized. Whenever new students and new teachers are added, new books should be tried, new art forms introduced, and new interrelationships established. Sometimes a humanities course will be discontinued when key teachers leave the school for greener pastures and other teachers are unable or unwilling to move out of their single subject sanctuary. Even when the same teaching team is continued from year to year, current events and the desire to move in different directions should dictate new approaches in humanistic studies. Unless change is specifically built into the humanities curriculum, the innovative features of the program can quickly become a new wall that blocks other reforms.

THE JOHN HAY FELLOWS PROGRAM

Most of the courses outlined below were placed in motion as a result of experiences school teachers and administrators enjoyed as participants in the John Hay Fellows Program in the humanities. Funded by the John Hay Whitney Foundation from 1952 to 1959, and in the main by the Ford Foundation until 1966, the John Hay Fellows Program, superbly directed for nine years by Dr. Charles R. Keller, was a unique experiment based on faith in people. The Program's goals and actions emphasized the humanities. It believed that:

> ... in all times, but especially in ours, men need an inner strength derived from a reverence for life and a continuing dedication to those ideals which afford dignity to man's existence. Although each person must develop this strength in his own way, he can be aided by a sensitive appreciation of the great heritage of human experience known as the humanities, the record of what men over the centuries have felt, thought, created, and done in their unceasing quest for the good life.[1]

Fellows in the year program were free to take whatever courses they wished at one of six universities associated with the Foundation. Opportunities for independent study and for an exchange of

---

[1]John Hay Fellows year fellowship brochure, 9 Rockefeller Plaza, New York, New York 10020.

ideas with other Fellows and with members of the university faculties were encouraged. In the Summer Humanities Institutes participants enrolled for morning seminars which dealt with the reading and discussion of several significant books. In addition, courses in aspects of philosophy, history, literature, music, art, and special programs were available. Never were tests or grades or credits given. Never was it necessary to check on the Fellows. Participants involved themselves in the Program because they wanted to study. Learning was for learning's sake. Dr. Keller, in the four Summer Humanities Institutes held each July, and in the year-long programs as well, gave each Fellow an opportunity to become immersed in humanistic studies. When they returned to their schools and classrooms, the Fellows were inspired to develop indigenous humanities programs.

By no means is the list exhaustive. Represented are some of the varieties of humanities courses found by Socrates Lagios and Robert Horne, teachers at Concord-Carlisle High School, Concord, Massachusetts, when preparing an overview of such programs.[2] Here too are courses based on other sources. In the light of our constantly changing world situation, one would be disappointed if the programs at the schools listed below are today an exact duplicate of what was devised some years ago.

Wisconsin High School, Madison, Wisconsin

A survey of the arts in historical context, open to all senior high school students. Painting, sculpture, architecture, music and drama are studied in six units:

The Renaissance	Neo-Classical	Modern Period
Baroque	Romantic	Contemporary Directions

Students' research papers are run off on ditto masters so that all students can discuss and keep reports.

Wheatley School, Old Westbury, New York
The junior year English course for all students includes the

[2]Robert Horne and Socrates Lagios, "An Overview of Humanistic Programs Throughout the Country," in *The English Leaflet,* ed. James T. Lape (P.O. Box 246, Wellesley, Mass., 1964), pp. 39-57.

relationship of this discipline to music, art, philosophy, history and the physical and biological sciences. Four themes are followed during the year: "Is There A Pattern?" "Interpersonal Communications Problems in Modern Society," "Man in Conflict," and "The Individual in Search of His Identity."

Traverse City High School, Traverse City, Michigan

A chronological approach illustrating major ideas in the history of Western thought. Literature, philosophy and art are stressed. Taught in three semesters as an elective to any junior or senior. The concept of man theme is illustrated within each epoch studied.

St. Louis Park High School, St. Louis, Missouri

A thematic design for bright seniors. Eighteen required selections include volumes from the Great Books Series. Film programs are also scheduled. Class pattern includes reading a book, writing an analysis of the content, and group discussion in a conference-style atmosphere.

Springfield High School, Springfield, Vermont

A senior year course replaces English and social studies for the non-college-bound students. Language, literature, history, art and music are integrated under a team approach.

Scarsdale High School, Scarsdale, New York

Courses offered to 30 able seniors on the basis of high reading scores and personal maturity. The humanities are viewed through the considerations of subject, elements, medium, style, function, and judgment. Two rooms are set aside as viewing, reading, and listening areas.

Richmond Public Schools, Richmond, Virginia

Several approaches have been developed: one program involves a class of juniors and seniors scheduled for three days a week conducted by teachers of philosophy, art and music. A second involves two art teachers who supplement the World History program by introducing related elements of art. George Wythe

High School offers a twelfth grade humanities course entitled "The Emergence of Man," taught by four teachers—English, art, music and history.

Neenah and Appleton High Schools, Neenah and Appleton, Wisconsin

A series of evening seminars for students from both schools in conjunction with local college professors leading discussions. Topics include Modern Poetry, The Novel, Music for the Listener, Sculpture and Architecture. No credits offered.

Mt. Lebanon High School, Pittsburgh, Pennsylvania

A free elective for all seniors in which Satire, Classicism, and Romanticism are discussed as movements that pervade all art forms. Use of various church musicians, both vocal and organ, and field trips to churches and other buildings to study symbolism and architecture.

Milne School, Albany, New York

An elective for bright seniors includes a team of four teachers who concentrate on the masterpieces of literature, music, painting, sculpture, and architecture. The full year course meets every day; the five periods available are usually divided into two literature, two music and one of visual arts.

Long Beach Unified School District, Long Beach, California

A chronological survey of the arts for bright students. Art, music, literature and drama are studied as expressions of man's culture. Weekly schedule includes a lecture on Monday, a field trip or viewing of art forms on Tuesday, student research on Wednesday and Thursday, and a discussion period on Friday.

Garfield High School, Seattle, Washington

Cultural patterns are the developing units in line with the socio-economic nature of the student population (1/3 Negro, 1/3 Oriental, 1/3 Caucasian): 1. Roots of Man (Intuitive and Cultural Man); 2. Nature of Man (Man, The Reasoner); 3. Future of Man (Man, The Dreamer).

Fairfield Public Schools, Fairfield, Connecticut

Questions such as "What Is Justice?" and "Is the Universe Ruled by Fate or Chance?" serve as the backdrop for a team taught humanities course which includes philosophy, literature, art, drama, and music for non-college-bound junior and senior students. Film, and other visual arts, as well as independent study are part of the course.

Abington High School, Abington, Pennsylvania

An elective course for able senior high school students introduces six philosophic and religious movements of our day—Existentialism, Marxism, Freudianism, Catholicism, Judaism, and Christianity. In each area students are asked how the movement influenced art, music and literature. Students keep "journals" of experiences.

MOVING THE FINE ARTS FROM THE MINORS TO THE MAJORS

Humanities courses provide a special blessing. They enable academically bound high school students to be reintroduced to the arts. In virtually every humanities program listed above, the disciplines of art and music are involved. Only rarely can a college preparatory student find time in the typically structured school schedule for courses in the arts. The five majors—history, English, science, mathematics, and foreign language—plus physical education, occupy all the available time.

Ask a cultured person why a school should include the arts in its curriculum and you will be informed that they are part of one's education for life. The arts constitute another language of communication; they express our joys, our fears, our hopes and our sorrows. They tell us about ourselves and others and present beauty and ugliness in ways other disciplines cannot. When man feels unable to cope with the pollutions in our lives, with the threat of atomic annihilation, with overpopulation, then the shapes and sounds of his art show through the mask of these anxieties. They provide new illuminations for an indifferent or hostile world.

Unfortunately the arts also provide another example of how far the theory is from the practice. Music and art are considered and treated not as major subjects but as minors. Many label them frills. The music and art we do permit to be taught in our secondary schools are primarily performance oriented. Rarely are students permitted to study the structure and history, or given the option to create their own music. The idea that students should have originality in handling sounds is not allowed to interfere with the main function of the school band, orchestra and choral groups—to perform. Of course the performing arts should perform. But to limit these disciplines to performance is to deny students the insights that come when a work is understood as well as played.

In nursery schools and in kindergarten, music and art are often freewheeling, eclectic classes which youngsters enjoy. But when the students move into formal schooling they are regimented to copy rather than create. Technical proficiency may be stressed for poster contests in art, and in music for half-time entertainment at football games, but seldom is the study of the arts approached as an extension of life's boundaries, as a means of expression and clarification of experiences.

Music and art courses that do exist in high schools have served far too often as dumping grounds for students with limited academic ability. The competition for selection to the college of one's choice makes academically oriented students extremely reluctant to drop a major subject requirement for a cultural program in music or art. And conventional wisdom relegates the student with no great spark for foreign languages or advanced academic courses to courses in the arts. Exposing these students to the disciplines of music and art is commendable but the courses are generally designed and function as "appreciation" subjects. Skills and creative thought are subordinated to passive, often boring, activities of listening, watching, and repeating. Appreciation should come from understanding, and not the other way around. Students have commented that the main difference between Art I and Art II in secondary school is the number.

The music our students do hear in school today does not resemble the sounds they understand and enjoy outside in their real world. Most schools have simply blocked out the contemporary music idiom of teenagers. We have only to hear their musical message to know how to communicate with them. The words used by Simon and Garfunkel, The Incredible String Band, the Beatles and others spell out in solid rock tones what students find interesting, vital, and worthwhile. Love, peace, growing up, loneliness, traveling, self-understanding, rebellion, and humor are some of the constant themes.

But contemporary art and music do not fit our concept of what the arts should include and so we teach a language that is out of tune with the tempo of the times. Not that rock music needs the school to give it a seal of approval. The irony of the sad situation in which school music is divorced from its contemporary idiom is that never has music been a more popular communicator for the young. Clive Barnes, the *New York Times'* dance and drama critic, considers rock music one of the most prevalent cultural trends of the past decade and, sociologically, the most interesting. "It is no coincidence," states Mr. Barnes, " that there is in a rock concert an element both of a sporting event and of religious celebration . . . it might occasionally be thought of as vicarious and surrogate hymns for people without an organized God."[3]

High school students are hungry for schools to give them more technical know-how in the playing of instruments, in the juxtapositioning of sounds. What young people do not want are judgments. And that is practically all the schools offer the students. After all, as someone observed, rock music is "raucous, rebellious, irreverent, out-of-tune, and unavailable in standard arrangements for marching band and mixed glee club." But even though music educators reject youth's music, rock will not go away.

Contemporary music and art have roots in our past. Students need to see the continuities as well as the discontinuities in their music and art world with the world they inherited. If we are to take seriously John Dewey's belief that learning is enhanced when students are exposed to new educational insights by taking them from where they are, the current musical and art idioms should serve as an effective starting point. Humanities courses are uniquely structured to provide such links. These disciplines can be blended with the other subjects in a humanities curriculum. The only fall-out will be at the expense of subject compartmentalization, an expense which students and teachers involved in these integrated programs seem eager to accept.

---

[3]*The New York Times,* July 5, 1969, Sec. 4, p. 22.

PHOTOGRAPHY, FILM AND TELEVISION—
OUR NEGLECTED DISCIPLINES

Music and art are tolerated as minors in the school curriculum. The newest arts—photography, film and television—have fared even worse: They have been virtually ignored as disciplines. A school has only six or seven hours each day in which to educate children. Majority faculty thinking would classify the newest media as entertainment and time cannot be "wasted" from the written word or drill work for amusements. That photography, film and television have a legitimacy of their own is not considered. Only a relative handful of the currently entrenched school personnel know enough about the new media to see their possibilities for learning.

Where film is used by teachers, too often it becomes a substitute for teaching or a break between units. Seldom do film, photography, and television serve as springboards for learning. Even in the wealthiest school districts, technological problems make the use of audio-visual equipment a less than ideal situation. Telling the students becomes easier and more certain than having a film re-create an episode or introduce a new idea. Students may remember the film version longer but the inevitable breakdown of audio-visual technology frustrates too many teachers.

Students are fully aware that the film does not count when determining grades. Once the lights go out, students reason that the teacher no longer knows, or cares, who is paying attention. The thinking processes stop, education ends, and sleep or entertainment begins. Of course, learning can be entertaining; of course hundreds of excellent educational films are available to intensify learning. But students need to be prepared for an instructional film if optimum results are anticipated. And teachers should preview a film as they preview a book before presenting it to the class. But the exigencies and excuses of poor school equipment and lost time make the typical audio-visual program something considerably less than an instructive experience.

Film and photography as an art form have gripped the younger generation in spectacular ways. Both Hollywood and the off-Hollywood movie industry have seized the opportunity to expose and exploit the medium primarily for box-office gold. We are in a new film age despite, or perhaps because of television. The film frontier with its probing lenses, intricate cameras, and fantastic experiments in motion, color, shapes and images is integrating the mental and the visceral in a totally new package. For young people the excitement of film movement or, as in photography, the freezing of movement, is a tantalizing prospect; it is contemporary; it is theirs. We need to teach students how to view films with more understanding and critical insight. We need to help them develop an appreciation of the techniques of cinematography. We need to bring this discipline into the mainstream of school life. Unfortunately, our schools are unprepared to capitalize on this student interest. Nor are we prepared to treat the new media as disciplines. Instead we disparage or ignore; we explain away the media by sticking to the tried and the tired. We stay with tradition. As a result, formal education makes scant use of the many means of communication which society at large finds indispensable. Television is a prime example of educational neglect. What we teach and the way we teach children in our schools differ much too much from the way they learn in the real out-of-school world.

Someone has observed that we have two kinds of foolish educators. One insists that if it is old, it is good; the other affirms if it is new, it is better. The mass media, like books, blackboards, overhead projectors and other impedimenta, will not create instant education. But film, photography and television are no longer toys. They have an artistry, a discipline, an expansion of meaning which school people must incorporate as part of the learning process. To fail to do so is to invite the legitimate student cry for relevancy.

THE ARTS AND THE HUMANITIES

Fortunately a humanities curriculum can encompass the mass media and the arts as disciplines in their own right, and as a forge with the major subjects. For example, a music teacher working with an English teacher can show the similarity of structure in the arts by having students listen to the first movement of Schubert's *Unfinished Symphony* as they follow a skeleton score. Parallels between the sonata-allegro form and literature are drawn: the exposition compared with an author's introduction of his leading characters in a novel. Students then discover for themselves how the first musical theme might be compared to the introduction of the hero, the second to the heroine, and so on. Soon music becomes a story in sound. And the sounds of the city can be shown to have musical overtones. In another humanities program the music and art teachers join the class when the social studies teacher discusses the mood of Russia under the Tsar. Moussorgsky's *Pictures at an Exhibition* is played and the art teacher shows Hartmann's pictures—the inspiration for Moussorgsky's music. The music and words of Arlo Guthrie's *Alice's Restaurant,* the hit records of the Beatles, The Rolling Stones, Simon and Garfunkel and the Broadway show *Hair* provide another kind of social message that students wish to discuss.

Unfortunately most of us have been taught to think only in words, to intellectualize. The use of space, shape, color, and object relationships as a way of adding new dimensions to thinking is not part of our working repertoire as teachers. Visual expression as a means of communication is far older than the written word. To ask the artist to verbalize the meaning of his painting or his sculpture is to dilute the very purpose of his creative effort. The old cliché that if an artist wanted to use words he would not be an artist is absolutely true. Art has the power to communicate, to build a bridge between human beings in directions other disciplines cannot reach. The artist can show us not just what he sees but the way he sees. In that moment the viewer senses what it is to be the artist. Thus Rembrandt's Holland comes alive and personal when we examine his paintings. And Picasso explained that art was the lie that revealed a greater truth.

Uncoupling life's mysteries through the arts is what Joseph Conrad discovered and described in his preface to *Nigger of the Narcissus:*

> ... the artist appeals to that part of our being which is not dependent on wisdom: to that in us which is a gift and not an acquisition—and, therefore, more permanently enduring. He speaks to our capacity for delight and wonder, to the sense of mystery surrounding our lives; to our sense of pity, and beauty, and pain; to the latent feeling of fellowship with all creation—and to the subtle but invincible conviction of solidarity in dreams, in joy, in sorrow, in aspirations, in illusions, in hope, in fear, which

binds men to each other, which binds together all humanity—the dead to the living and the living to the unborn.[4]

This is the dimension of art and artistry which our schools have denied students.

There are countless examples of how schools could tap this stimulating resource. One of the most exciting, provocative films to trigger thinking and develop creative insights is the Saul Bass animated and live production produced by the Kaiser Aluminum Corporation called "Why We Create." The National Football League's six minute color film "Headcracker" is a beautiful blending of music, dance, drama and technology. Edward Steichen's photographic exhibition *The Family of Man* provides an unforgettable experience and affirmation of humanity's oneness. The power of photography in peace and war is an accepted procedure in life. But our schools continue to place almost exclusive stress on the written word.

Unfortunately few school systems have recognized the value of allowing a fine arts teacher sufficient time from athletic and holiday program rehearsals to develop a humanities program with colleagues in other disciplines. Instead, the fine arts and the other disciplines lead their own separate lives in this golden age of unconnected teaching.

HUMANITIES AS EXPERIMENTATION

Because the humanities is still a new subject in our schools, teachers are relatively free to experiment with different approaches, different techniques, different emphases. No biblical testament has yet been devised which all students must memorize and regurgitate on an examination.

From first grade to twelfth grade and beyond, the traditional teaching pattern has come to mean covering so many pages in a textbook, completing so many chapters in a curriculum guide, giving tests, recording grades and moving on to the next assign-

---

[4]Joseph Conrad, "The Nigger of the Narcissus," in *Tales of Land and Sea* (New York: Hanover House, 1953), p. 106.

ment. In the process of mastering facts, dates, theorems, and vocabulary lists, the enduring values of justice, freedom, virtue, beauty and truth somehow get lost in the shuffle. And the excitement, the juices of a discipline, are distilled. Both students and teachers concentrate instead on the dull bare bones, the skeleton of each subject. "Teachers teach, students listen," is the conventional formula. But learning should be more than a spectator sport. Visit any school between class periods and the din of student involvement with one another is all to obvious. Then the bell rings, the students troop to class, and soon from too many rooms we hear only the teacher's authoritarian voice.

In a humanities program where all learning is not preordained, students have opportunities to be heard, to become involved, to find out for themsleves, to ask their own questions, to feel free to make their own discoveries and their own mistakes. One reason why modern mathematics has captured the interest of more young people today than in the past is that the students are expected to discover the principles of multiplication rather than to learn the multiplication tables by rote. Teachers in a humanities program must have the competence to make learning a detective story rather that a catechism; they must know when to have students zoom in on a topic and when to take a sweeping panoramic view. The worst sin a humanities teacher can commit is to follow an even, monotonous pattern of coverage which includes everything and emphasizes nothing. Dr. Keller has observed that a successful humanities program is determined often before it begins, when the staff decides what to exclude as well as what to include. He advocates a man-centered, idea-centered, experience-centered, interdisciplinary education; this in place of the present-day information-gathering-centered, fact-centered, course-centered, subject centered, grade-getting-centered, bell-interrupted variety.[5] Man-centered education gives young people—and their teachers— opportunities to study man in all his relationships: with the past, with the present, with himself, with his fellow human beings, with his physical environment, with space, with his gods. "It is

---

[5] Charles R. Keller, "Toward A New American History," in *The Bulletin of the National Association of Secondary School Principals* (Washington, D.C.: April 1970), LIV, pp. 29-30.

imperative to put the emphasis on man," Dr. Keller insists. "Only man who has studied man can live as man."[6]

WHAT VALUES SHOULD WE STRESS?

If man becomes the fulcrum, the humanities programs in our schools will be less a sum of knowledge than a way of thinking and being, a search for values and a rejection of dogmatism. Values are never really taught, they are caught. To develop sound values and humane character in our students, a faculty needs to demonstrate these attitudes both in their philosophy and in their lives.

Every school system has a statement of its values and goals. They are found in the student and teacher handbooks distributed by the school administration. Often they are nailed in an impressive frame along the main school corridor. What are these values? In first place, generally, are the skill values of reading, writing, and arithmetic. Such values as a belief in the United States of America, a faith in democracy, respect for property and human rights, tolerance, good health, and character development will also be listed as part of a school's philosophy.

Why then do we as a school in society do so poorly in developing a broad area of shared beliefs in something nobler than material satisfactions? The answer will be found in examining our heroes and our priorities. Student values are learned and embedded not from the memorization of words or events in school; they come from working and identifying with people around them. Emerson has observed that a man is what he thinks about all day long and "no institution will be better than the institutor."[7] Young people in particular, who seem to be attracted to the latest thing, seek models to emulate, models of what man at his best can be. But in our society and in our schools they find in the main a competitive struggle for personal power rather than a cooperative spirit for the public good.

Some students reject materialism and radicalize themselves in a commune style of thinking and action. The over-thirty generation,

---

[6]*Ibid.*, p. 31.

[7]Ralph Waldo Emerson, "Character," *Essays* (Boston: Houghton Mifflin Co., 1883), p. 100.

the mass media, indeed the entire Establishment, is suspected and excluded. Young radicals dress differently, find cleanliness and godliness to be irrelevant, and develop a new dress and philosophical conformity of their own. Some students join "the movement" for the fun and excitement and shock value of trying something new. An increasing number of our young people, disenchanted with the hypocrisy between democratic preaching and practice, are raising serious questions about armaments, hunger, overpopulation, and values. When the school and the home refuse to face the reality of their questions, these radical youth move on to their own revolutionary answers.

Most students are not radicals. Like their parents, they are swayed by the Madison Avenue pied pipers. Too many girls consider it a sign of womanhood when they dye their eyelids green, their nails red, and their hair yellow. Too many boys think they are men when they own a car, smoke a cigar (or pot), and have sex appeal. Most students are more concerned with the clothes than the books they need for college. We may bemoan such surface values but these are the adult cultural images which they see advertised and which they copy.

Properly implemented, a humanistic approach to learning will widen the student's horizon; it will help give him a moral view of man. The contrast between our social segregation and distrust and our technological achievements has become another cliché. Our civilization has shown itself far more willing to underwrite scientific explorations than explorations in human understanding. Humanities programs in our schools will not, by themselves, reverse this pattern. Nor can the humanities offer any panacea, any miracle pill, for strengthening social and ethical values. The humanities cannot send rockets to distant planets, it cannot conquer cancer, it cannot guarantee happiness. We study the humanities because we believe it is good for the soul.

In Laconia, New Hampshire, the Board of Education summoned Miss Eleanor Parker, a humanities teacher, and asked her to justify the inclusion of Harper Lee's *To Kill A Mockingbird* in the humanities program. Miss Parker replied:

> When I use this book, I look at my students and hope they and I will learn to be like Atticus Finch, to meet ignorance, hatred, prejudice, not with more ignorance, hatred, prejudice but with understanding, goodness, love . . .

Students respect Atticus because he is an adult who practices what he preaches. More than ever, today young people are questioning us as adults when our lives do not measure up to our words . . .

I have spent over half my life working with young people in school and in church and working with language, the miracle that makes us human. It is through language that we think, communicate, express our ideas, and transmit them down the years. Why study literature? Because it is one of the humanities—one of the ways by which man expresses his beliefs, his hopes, his understandings, without having to experience directly every aspect of life. It helps us to develop values, ideals, a sense of purpose . . .

I consider this book a superior source for such development because the basic idea is that prejudice poisons the mind, and that the only cure is understanding.[8]

The school board voted unanimously to continue the humanities program. This teacher's view of teaching is what the humanities is all about.

---

[8]Statement made by Miss Eleanor Parker at Board of Education meeting, Laconia, New Hampshire 03246, October 1964.

CHAPTER 3

Discovering and Developing
Human Potential in
a Humanistic Environment

A favorite story on the discovery and development of human potential deals with an elementary school student who chanced to pass a sculptor working on a slab of marble. The youngster watched the sculptor chipping away for some moments and then he continued his walk to school. On successive days the child observed the sculptor laboring on the marble in what appeared to be an aimless task. One day, the child stopped to examine the work and, to his astonishment, noticed that the face of President Lincoln was beginning to emerge. He turned to the sculptor and exclaimed, "How did you know that Lincoln was in that marble!"

TEACHER EXPECTATIONS AND STUDENT ACHIEVEMENT

In teaching the humanities, unlike sculpting, we cannot be certain that by chiseling away we can create a Lincoln. We do not have the precision instruments to determine how a child will develop. But we can attempt to lead our boys and girls to the threshold of their own minds. Each one of our students has within him capabilities of action and emotion and thought we never truly comprehend or reach. Humanity's possibilities are infinite. The influence of a teacher in awakening some of the many lives which slumber in our students is what makes teaching the humanities so exciting an experience.

Some teachers have a clear sense of direction in which to *make* their students move. They offer a set humanities curriculum. They have developed a standardized procedure; they have firm ground rules for success in class; they "process" students through their humanities courses. Many students have been educated to accept this type of restrictive classroom atmosphere in which the teacher hammers away until a lesson is learned. "Forced feeding" of knowledge is a time-worn educational procedure. Because children prefer play to work, the theory goes, they will naturally resist learning. To become educated requires strain and stress, a condition young people wish to avoid. The antidote: make mastery of knowledge a prerequisite for promotion to the goals youth really desire—adulthood status and freedom of choice.

Even in the primitive tribes, it is argued, children were required to undergo severe initiation rites before being accepted as full-fledged members of the community. Today we use the instrumentality of the school to accomplish similar functions.

That going to school should be fun is never seriously considered by educators who follow the forced feeding philosophy. Tests, assignments, grades, detention hall, and the principal's office are sharp weapons in the teacher's arsenal to compel learning. With such finely honed tools, students can be prodded to jump through the school's educational hoops. If they refuse they will fail, and entrance to the main arena of learning and living may never be reached. Since even the self-made man needs a basic education that includes a college degree these days, the majority of students follow the school pipers.

Other humanities teachers are less sanguine. Like Mark Hopkins, they see the student not as an empty mind to be filled but as a flame to be fed. The task of the humanities teacher, they believe, is to stir the fires, to provide the kindling for students to discover and develop their own possibilities. Once a student grasps the idea that he is responsible for his own education, that he should contribute as well as receive, his attitude toward school can assume a new positivism. He no longer is taught; he is learning. To be taught is passive, to learn is active. And rather than focus on a dreary playback each day of what all students know or have been forced to memorize, the emphasis, for these humanities teachers, is on exploring with students what they do not know. Teaching then no longer becomes simply a matter of learning what's right and what's wrong. Rather than a body of knowledge to be digested whole, this form of humanistic study utilizes knowledge as a means of understanding the actions or inactions of the students. Teachers therefore spend less time as evaluators and more time as diagnosticians,—and friends in learning. In such a school setting students are able to extend themselves. They develop confidence in the face of the unknown. Instead of waiting like oysters in the bay for the tide to flow in, the students are eager to start themselves.

The differences between the two forms of education, between knowledge mastery and self-mastery, need not be an irreparable cleavage. John Dewey maintained long ago that a deep and genuine concern for individual growth and fulfillment not only is compatible with but indeed demands an equally genuine concern for cognitive growth and intellectual discipline, for transmitting the cultural heritage of the society.[1] Unfortunately, in the overwhelming majority of schools the gravitational pull is toward either end of the educational spectrum. Seldom do we find the blending that Dewey correctly saw as essential.

DEVELOPING THE PROPER SCHOOL ATMOSPHERE

Schools fail students when the human expectation level is lowered. If the philosophy of the school board and the school administration is to teach the best and ignore the rest, the school teachers will learn soon enough that it is easier when working with

---

[1]John Dewey, *Experience and Education* (New York: Macmillan Co., 1953), p. 93. "But the achievements of the past provide the only means at command for understanding the present. Just as the individual has to draw in memory upon his own past to understand the conditions in which he individually finds himself, so the issues and problems of present *social* life are in such intimate and direct connection with the past that students cannot be prepared to understand either these problems or the best way of dealing with them without delving into their roots in the past."

students of apparent limited ability to "flunk them and forget them" or to "pass them along and get rid of them." If it is an honor to work with honor students in a humanities program and a punishment to be assigned to teach the other classes, the average and slow youngsters will not take long to realize that they are not wanted. And they will behave accordingly even if they are assigned to a humanities program of their own. Placing students in a humanities program can help develop new understandings and a higher quality of education. But the total school atmosphere generally has a more pervasive effect on student thought and attitudes than any single subject. Some teachers and some humanities courses do serve like an oasis in a desert for students. The refreshment and stimulation received in that single session each day may be enough to keep the students on the regular attendance rolls. Too often the remaining hours provide an eternity of boring, formal rituals. In a school where administrators and teachers are concerned with developing spontaneity, initiative, and wholesome curiosity in their students as well as critical thinking and intellectual discipline, the school atmosphere promoting such goals will permeate every phase of the school day.

Equal educational opportunity is not the same as equal education. All students may be enrolled in the same humanities class and have the same teacher. But if the teacher only calls on those students who are quick to grasp an idea, she will move along at a pace out of line with the needs of many. If a teacher demonstrates conscious or unconscious prejudice by not recognizing the upraised black or brown hand, she turns these students off as effective learners. Every student should be made to feel of equal worth as a human being in a democratically inspired school. But every student will be given unequal assistance—assistance that conforms with individual needs to nurture and develop human potential. Differentiated questioning and individualized instruction is what all students need and want.

Another example of the crucial importance of a humanistic school atmosphere in enhancing education: When the pressure to recognize the need for special programs for bright youngsters was in vogue during the early 1960s, a large school system in central New York State decided to take action. A bulletin was issued, duly signed by the school superintendent and approved with great fanfare by the board of education, that beginning immediately, all schools had to establish special classes for students with intelligence quotients over 120. The regulation was written on paper and obeyed on paper. In all schools but one, the high I.Q. students were grouped together and little more was actually done.

In all schools but one. A problem confronted the administration in this one school. Virtually the entire student body represented minority groups. Many were transients. Few had parents who could read and write English with facility. Not a single child in this entire school had an intelligence quotient over 120. For obvious reasons it was deemed impolitic to report that no students in this school were qualified to attend honor classes. So quite arbitrarily, a group of students was assigned to what was designated the honors section of the school.

When the schools in this city were visited, we discovered that with one exception the new honors classes were conducted and the material was covered in approximately the same way as the regular classes. But in the school where no students actually qualified for honor sections, the enthusiasm and stimulation of the students was a joy to behold. These boys and girls were working as though they actually were honor students. A wise school administrator and a teacher had informed them they were to be given special opportunities to learn. The students were never told that they were not very bright.

HUNTER COLLEGE HIGH SCHOOL

All students need to feel important. At Hunter College High School a 100 year heritage of great expectations from students and a reverence for learning provide a self-fulfilling prophecy in raising aspiration levels. In 1870, when Thomas Hunter persuaded the City Fathers to establish the first public and secondary school for girls in New York City, the school's tradition of respect for human excellence was inaugurated. This tradition remains strong. Located in the heart of New York City on the thirteenth and fourteenth floors of a block-long office building at 46th Street and Lexington Avenue, the school serves today as a laboratory for demonstration, research, and experimentation for its parent institution, Hunter College. From 1965 to 1969, the author served as the school's principal as well as professor of education. In 1970 he became director of both the Hunter College elementary and secondary schools.

WHY EXPERIMENTAL SCHOOLS?

Not a few members of the educational fraternity believe that it makes little sense to establish experimental schools. "Make a good idea operational in a typical school and then we may listen to your suggestions," they say. "The only realistic experimentation," the argument continues, "is the kind that takes place under normal conditions."

We educators are a conservative breed. Too many of us follow the axiom, "Never do anything for the first time." But in the real world of industry and the professions, innovative ideas are generally not developed full bloom in the main branch. Laboratories and research centers are recognized today as indispensable adjuncts of any forward moving enterprise. If we had waited until new educational experiments were first introduced in typical schools, many of the present technological and curricular changes in secondary education would not have been considered. Because laboratory schools are less burdened by political pressures, less inhibited by conservative traditions, and less worried about making mistakes, they are in a position to make new discoveries. If a laboratory school keeps at least one eye cocked on the implications of its innovative programs in the humanities and other areas for "regular" schools, the existence of such a special school seems eminently justified.

The final paragraph of the Hunter College High School's Philosophy and Objectives reads as follows:

> We are privileged to be in a school in which the principle that students and teachers should learn together is a practice and not just a promise; where students are prepared for leadership positions in their world of tomorrow by exercising leadership in their world of today; where intelligence is honored, service to others is expected and experimentation is a concomitant of school life.

By tradition, and by belief then, the academic program at Hunter College High School has four essential ingredients:

    1. intellectual integrity and rigor;

2. direction and focus determined by the entire school community;

3. faculty commitment and enjoyment of both students and subjects;

4. cooperative as well as competitive environment in which much is expected.

HUMAN SCHOOL PROBLEMS

All schools develop or inherit educational misfits and mistakes. On certain days school administrators can claim to have more than their fair share. Some students are so politically dedicated to revolutionizing the established school system that they have no time for academic toil. They become masters in using their talents to achieve at the minimum possible level. For many youngsters, emotional, psychological, economic or physical problems often make schooling completely irrelevant. Nor is this situation limited to students. Some of our younger teachers wish to make of each class an encounter or sensitivity group and are eager to dispense with all formal learning and traditions which have helped keep the entity of the school. Older teachers will fight just as resolutely to resist change because the old ways are more comfortable.

Parents constitute a special problem. A child is an extension of one's self. Few parents can be truly objective in assessing the strengths and weaknesses of their children. Depending on the parents' self-image, the usual procedure is to demand too much or too little from their children. And if parental expectations cannot or will not be fulfilled, the school becomes an easy scapegoat to explain failure.

Few "average" parents are really prepared to cope with truly gifted children. The tendency for these parents is to move in one of two extremes with their bright prodigies—either complete domination or complete neglect. When parents demand total conformity, the students often feel as though they are imprisoned. In a real sense, they are. A talented child requires more than the local newspaper, television and "G" films at the movie theater to keep her curiosity effervescent. When the teenager finally explodes from such a home environment she sometimes makes the school her whole life. More often the student rebels by refusing to do her school work. A youngster punishing her parents by deliberately failing her subjects is an old form of revenge.

Sometimes the bright student moves from the home and the school to the streets. She may become politically active and strive to help others, or become a revolutionary and join a commune to take action in ways not provided by the school. Sometimes the student will turn inward, live for the moment, and for herself. An increasing number are turning to drugs, mysticism, and the exotic religions. In most instances school then becomes extraneous, meaningless, an arm of the "Establishment." For such students, the more the school seeks to act *in loco parentis,* the more the student is alienated.

Most parents confronted with a bright child take the opposite posture. They follow a pattern of permissiveness and find it expedient to let the teenager do as she pleases. By no means is this policy limited to parents of the gifted! Young people may demand freedom from adult supervision and regulation but they really want and need some guidelines, directions and examples. When the home does not provide such advice and consent, the talented student often faces disastrous consequences in her personal relationships, and in school. A policy of everything goes soon leads to a situation in which everything is gone.

To teach bright students is a special privilege and a special challenge. These students want to learn. They have a sense of curiosity about the world. Nothing is taken for granted. "Why is a watt called a watt?" asks a seventh grader. Most of these youngsters believe that it is stupid not to do your homework because you do not get as much out of a lesson when you are unprepared. Since as high school students they travel light, their moralistic fervor and rectitude are at a higher pitch than at any other time in their lives. They are full of contradictions, joyous and serious, true believers and cynics. Because they are alert, because they read and see so much on their own, they bring to the classroom and to each other a liberality of experiences. In general, talented students are gregarious, questioning, stimulating, and exhausting.

STUDENTS OF LIMITED ABILITY IN A
HUMANITIES CURRICULUM

One of the numerous fallacious theories concerning the humanities is that such integrated programs must be limited to bright students. Of course, academically talented students will thrive in an academically oriented, challenging humanities curriculum. But what kinds of experiences should students of lesser academic ability receive? Objection may be raised to any cultural courses for senior high school students who read at a fifth or sixth grade level. What's needed, critics will insist, is a crash program in the basics if these young people are ever to cope with the written word.

Unfortunately by the time they reach high school, these youngsters have been turned off and tuned out. Inadequate reading methods, a lack of motivation and a reluctance on the part of many students to expose their ignorance have all contributed to make them non-readers. For these students, another dose of the traditional textbooks and the traditional teaching techniques simply will not do. By the time the non-academically oriented student reaches high school he has been made to feel dumb. No wonder so many secondary school students have no high regard for schooling. No wonder that nearly 25 percent of each age group decides not to suffer schooling until graduation. These students are acutely aware that without a high school diploma most vocational doors may be permanently closed. But they cannot or will not continue to experience failure and frustration with an unresponsive curriculum.

What do students of limited academic ability want and need? Above all, they want to feel good about themselves; they want to have positive self-concepts; they want to believe that they are worth listening to. Secondly, they hope that someone cares about them as human beings. They wish to belong to a group, a family, a community, a nation, to some organization bigger than themselves. Thirdly, they need to develop the skills and patience that will enable them to listen to other opinions, to learn how to weigh evidence, to make wise judgments. Because their attention spans may not be as sustained, as disciplined as other students', they need more variety in course content and procedures. Indeed all students, not just those with limited academic ability, now insist on these same goals. And the humanities, with its emphasis on the affective as well as the cognitive areas, with its use of the visual as well as the written word, offers an excellent method of providing such variety and substance. Humanities can substitute solid programs in literature, aesthetics, and current topics for the prevailing pattern of Minnie Mouse courses that neither teachers nor the non-academic students respect. Examples of racial tensions, war and peace movements, women's liberation programs, and the problems of hunger, overpopulation, and family relations will have meaning for the able as well as the academically limited students. The economic, social, and political causes for the War of the Roses or the War of 1812 will not.

When students of limited ability, when all students, leave our schools they should have come to believe in a value system that offers alternatives to revolution, looting, and mysticism as methods of seeking solutions to problems. A humanities curriculum is a most effective framework in which respect for the students as human beings is coupled with a program of studies offering perspective and purpose. Audio-visual aids, reading materials, levels of depth, and conceptual discussions will differ with different students, different teachers, and different communities. But the structure of the humanities curriculum with its goals and values based on individual self-worth, a sense of sharing, and a commitment to be a constructive member of the human race, is a program for all students in all schools.

TAKING PROFESSIONALISM SERIOUSLY

Although students of average or limited ability have generally been cowed to accept lackluster teaching or leave school, talented youngsters can and often do use their intellectual gifts to destroy mediocre teachers. Bright students will not allow "busy work" to occupy their time. If the teacher will not or cannot change to a program that offers challenge and interest, the students will soon change the teacher. To be a permanent teacher with any level of students should require a special measure of commitment—a commitment to remain a scholar in one's subject, a commitment to work with students in the variety of in-and-out-of-school activities, a commitment to know the students as human beings.

Students should respect most of the faculty as friends rather than solely as teachers. Such teacher commitments are needed when working in any school. When dealing with bright students they constitute minimum essentials.

Commitment and professionalism are words greeted with scorn and cynicism in the educational world today. Nonetheless they still apply. No teacher should be required to report at a certain hour each morning and stay until a specified time each afternoon. A professional person will do what is right without demeaning external restraints. No teacher should sign in or out at any time. A teacher has the responsibility of notifying her department chairman if she will be late or absent. The administration need not presume to be a better judge of how a teacher can make the best use of time out of class. Professional activity which will help students is not confined to the school building. College professors follow this procedure but the policy of treating teachers as professionals has not trickled down to the public schools. Where such trust has been demonstrated in a few public schools the attendance record is gratifyingly high. Nor do the majority of teachers in these schools rush out of the building once formal classes are concluded each day.

PRESSURES ON SCHOOLS

School pressures are constant and growing all over the country. Students read the demands made by college radicals and immediately incorporate the ideas as their own. Black, Chicano, and Puerto Rican students demand special studies. Jewish, Chinese, and Italian minorities demand special foreign language courses. The flag salute and the singing of the national anthem are protested. Holding large assembly programs is a risk fewer and fewer administrators are willing to take. Students wish to decide for themselves whether to attend specific classes. In turn, the subject departments insist that students should spend more time studying their respective disciplines.

All department chairmen and their staffs zealously guard their domains of influence. Departments wish to set their own rules on what constitutes acceptable work, on what a report card grade means, on classroom procedures, homework, and professional conduct. Each department is entitled to its own integrity but the cost for such independence in terms of school uniformity and cooperation comes very high. A curriculum committee composed of representatives from each discipline is one of the more effective procedures to make Solomonic decisions when departmental autonomy or curriculum change comes in conflict with others. In some schools both the chairman and one other teacher in the same discipline are committee members. A few schools permit student representatives to attend and vote. All resolutions passed by the curriculum committee are then referred to the entire faculty and to the student government for final approval.

The pressures outside the school are even more frustrating. The schools have suddenly been "discovered" by the politically active community groups. From the extreme right to the extreme left, including all shades of opinion in-between, the cry is to remake the school into a new force, a new function. The school as an ivy-covered house of learning standing apart from social pulls and pressures is no longer a tenable posture. Unfortunately neither the men nor the machines of education are organized to deal effectively with political pressure points.

Our schools are in the position of the young man who failed to please his mother no matter how many different girls he brought home as prospective brides. One girl was not pretty enough, another not bright enough, still another too bright. So it went. The young man finally thought he found a solution. He brought home a young lady who was just like his mother. She looked like his mother, talked like his mother, even walked like his mother. But he was still in trouble. His father did not like her.

When a faculty receives letters like the following from graduates, the community can feel certain that at least for some a humanistic school environment prevails:

> We have been comparing notes, my roommates and I, and I am struck by the difference in their school preparation and mine . . . Not so much in subjects for we seem to have taken similar basic programs. But they considered going to school to be a chore, a thing they had to go through in order to get into college.
>
> With us, going to school was fun. Always—or nearly always—there was an excitement about learning in our school that made getting up each morning a great experience . . . I have concluded

that our whole school atmosphere was responsible for the difference between their education and mine.[2]

The atmosphere in which human potential is nurtured does make the essential difference in schools. If students and faculty are trusted, trusted to really make the *important* decisions, trusted to feel responsible and responsibility, they will respond in kind.

Atmosphere is not created or introduced overnight. We cannot transplant an artificial environment and assume that all the other organs and muscles of the school body will continue to function normally. It takes time, infinite patience, and continued confidence in humanity. For a school administrator and a board of education, it also requires a thick skin. It means developing an attitude on priorities, on when and how tests should be administered, on listening to and sharing with the young, on expecting much, and on never despairing over short-range failure. It involves having a faculty and administration who are honest with themselves and one another. Finally, it means having an innate dissatisfaction with the status quo no matter how adequate or quiet the school situation. In too many communities, one irate letter to the board of education causes a panic, two, an emergency closed door meeting, and three, absolute chaos.

By osmosis, and by example, students will learn to flourish as human beings in a school where an atmosphere of trust prevails. In such a school a humanities curriculum is embodied in the totality of the student's day, in the extra-curricular as well as curricular activities. In such a school a humanities curriculum may not be necessary; the students will be immersed in the humanity of living all day long. In such a school a teacher's influence would be generated by competence rather than position. And students would have as much freedom as they have the capacity to handle—perhaps even a little more free choice than they can handle, in order to stretch their capacities. Such a utopian dream will not be actualized today or tomorrow. We all live in an imperfect world, and in an imperfect school environment. Until our school and our society re-create heaven on earth, humanities programs can serve as a Jacob's ladder. Hopefully the humanities courses will help us climb up, rather than climb down.

---

[2]Jane Taylor to school principal, November 14, 1969.

CHAPTER 4

Utilizing the School and the Community
As a Humanities Laboratory

THE SENIOR SLUMP

No person who has occupied either side of a teacher's desk needs a lengthy explanation of what is commonly called "the senior slump." By the time a student becomes a high school senior, the educational institution offers few surprises. Patterns of classes, homework, sports, clubs, cafeteria and study hall rituals are now dull routines. For the few seniors who do exercise leadership positions, the final year may continue to hold interest; for the majority who put in time until graduation, the senior year is a bore.

And boredom breeds problems. In schools where more than a majority are college bound, students can usually be kept in rein until the ides of April. Not wishing to jeopardize college admissions by cutting classes, most students grumble silently. Similarly, seniors who are dependent on school officials for vocational recommendations recognize the wisdom of discretion. But once a student has received a letter of acceptance from the college of his choice, or from an employer, all manner of hell can be expected to break loose.

Students are then no longer willing to remain timid and tense. Absences and latenesses increase at geometric rates. School principals and superintendents can use the ultimate weapon. On grounds of poor citizenship, administrators can deny an uncooperative or unruly student the right to receive a diploma and to graduate. But few officials have the temerity to take so drastic a step. After all, the student will then stay in school another year and cause even more trouble! Furthermore, citizenship is too amorphous a term to permit a definitive statement of its violation.

By May and June, for many students school becomes a hostile way station, a pause that depresses before graduation, a prison in which you count the hours to freedom. In such an atmosphere even the best teachers have difficulty convincing students to read and prepare work. The senior slump begins.

When confronted with this record of nonattendance and nonachievement, student reaction follows a predictable pattern:

"I have been going to school for thirteen years. I want a rest."

"What difference does it make? I've been accepted by a college. Even if I fail, I'm in."

"I am sick and tired of learning things because you tell me I need it for college or a job. I've done what you wanted, now I want to do what I like and not what I need."

"School is a prison. I can have much more fun and learn more, too, by doing what I think worthwhile in the city."

Even the "conformists," even the students who find school to their liking, experience little incentive to be excited about their final school year—except that soon they will leave.

CHANGING THE SCHOOL ROUTINE

Only the minority of students actively involved in athletic competition, a drama festival, student government, a special independent study program, or a prom continue to come to school willingly. Since most seniors have little appetite to be fed the same basic academic program and class pattern they experienced in the previous years, and since teachers are most unhappy to face disgruntled students day after day, it should not require too much prodding to convince the faculty to break the senior slump by altering the traditional routine of classes.

Actually, the senior slump virus has infected students in the lower school years as well. An increasing number of boys and girls are attempting to shorten their school apprenticeships by attending summer sessions and by taking additional required subjects during the regular academic year. In doing so, they reduce the traditional four year high school sequence for grades nine through twelve by a full year. Nearly 25 percent of the high school students elect a different path. They leave. More than one school critic has insisted that these students do not drop out; they are forced out. The rush to escape from high school can be attributed to many "outside" causes: a desire to leave home, to enter college, to make money. Whatever the reason, the climate of the high school is not sufficiently stimulating to convince these students that laboring at learning is worth four full years. Some students should leave home and high school as soon as possible. Most students remain in the community school no matter how dull the daily assignments.

But the school need not be a dull, joyless place! If the educational system is man and woman made, it can be changed by these practitioners into an exciting learning environment.

A procedure virtually guaranteed to change the entire school is to have one period each month last an entire day. In October, for example, all classes meeting the first period would continue through the afternoon. On a day in November, the students and teachers in second period classes would meet continuously during all the school hours. In December the third period would be used, etc. Forcing teachers and students to face each other for six or seven consecutive hours will really shake up traditional approaches. The foreign language teacher, the mathematics teacher, and the physical education teacher, to take but three examples, cannot possibly continue to teach for an entire school day in the routine pattern pursued during the regular 40 or 50 minute period. Alternative schedules must be developed. Teachers and students with imagination will seize upon the increased time to visit a factory, or see a dramatic production, or view a film, discuss its special features, and then watch the film again after larger insights have been gained. Librarians have taken students to a metropolitan library and to a book bindery. Physical education teachers have had their students try the obstacle course at a neighboring military installation. A business education teacher can arrange a tour of commercial accounting and secretarial offices.

The beauty of this change-of-pace is that moving classes out of the school does not interfere with other academic programs. And once new community-wide approaches to teaching are tried, the log jam is broken on still other innovative ideas. Having the same students in the same subject for an entire day becomes an infectious device which triggers fresh thinking on the best use of the traditional 40 or 50 minute period as well.

Meeting individual differences by encouraging independent study and community work programs, having mini courses with solid content, bringing parents and students into curriculum discussions and decisions, and permitting students to serve as teachers are some other ways to keep the school organization from falling asleep.

Several schools have reversed the curriculum process completely for a one or two week period each term and have had the students devise the course of study. Students have called this period "The Ideal School Week." Such subjects as "Discovering My Community" in which an architect parent served as teacher to help see the city with fresh eyes, and "Discovering Myself" led by another parent who was a psychologist were suggested. A history teacher used the two week period to offer a course on his hobby, "Vintage Automobiles." Other teachers, parents, and students taught courses in film-making, pollution control, anthropology, rug weaving, etc. Students elected whatever courses they wished to follow. Although attendance was not compulsory, most schools found that they had far fewer absences than during the regular class sessions. The "Ideal School Week" change of pace is fun, is stimulating, is meaningful.

SENIOR SEMINARS

A more dramatic procedure that has proven successful is ending all senior classes some six weeks to two months prior to the close of the school year. The seniors are then enrolled in what has been termed the Senior Seminar. Schools can readily follow a similar procedure for other high school classes as well.

Actually the faculty should introduce the students to the Senior Seminar idea no later than January. Students would then be informed that for the final months of their school year they will have an opportunity to work independently and in depth on some aspect of twentieth century life not generally selected for intensive study in the traditional curriculum. Instead of being forced to attend classes in school, they can find their learning experiences in the community, by themselves as part of a tutorial program, and in other ways. Areas of the students' personal interests should be suggested. Teachers freed during the Senior Seminars from holding regular classes are now available to serve as student advisors. Meetings with students to discuss their individual programs would be scheduled by the advisors either singly or in small groups, one day each week. On a second school day all students would return to school to present progress reports, to attend to special class and school-wide concerns, to participate in assembly programs, and the like. The three remaining days would be available for project work in the community. A student's schedule could take this form during the Senior Seminar:

Mon.:	Community Work and/or Study	
Tues.:	A.M.	Small Group Sessions with student advisor
	P.M.	Individual Conferences
Wed.:	Community Work and/or Study	
Thur.:	A.M.	Special school-wide and class activities, assemblies, etc.
	P.M.	Large group Sessions—Progress Reports and Discussion
Fri.:	Community Work and/or Study	

Although students clamor for freedom to do their own thing, when freedom is extended many youngsters are frequently at a loss to make choices. Instead of developing their own ideas the tendency is to turn to the faculty either instinctively or fearfully and ask, "What do you suggest?" We have indoctrinated our students only too well! After eleven years of listening to the authority figure in the classroom for direction and discipline, many high school students find it most difficult to suddenly cope with liberty. Freedom of choice in education must begin not at age sixteen but at age six. Of course young people need guidelines and structure. But to deny them any real self-initiative, to offer them only a single acceptable pattern to follow until the senior high school years, is to virtually destroy students' ability to deal intelligently with democratic decision-making.

Failure in the past, however, is no legitimate excuse for not attempting fresh efforts. Participatory democracy can be learned at any age. The Senior Seminar can encourage students to make choices if proper preparations are initiated. Teachers in a variety of disciplines as well as citizens in community agencies should be invited to offer suggestions when the students are assembled in January for the initial Senior Seminar session. To wait until April or May is to foreclose on many project opportunities. Moreover students must have time to make explorations and contacts on their own.

Good sense as well as good public relations dictate that all the teachers and the whole community be invited to suggest suitable seminar programs. The following letter could be sent to the entire school staff and placed in the local newspaper:

> If you know of seminar opportunities for students, where they can work and learn and give service with individuals in various fields, please let us know.
>
> The students would benefit greatly by being exposed to both professional and lay people in a variety of areas—publishing, politics, research, museums, college, the arts, advertising, social welfare, the theater, commerce, etc.

One of the teachers freed from classes because of the seminar program can be asked to serve as coordinator in assembling the suggestions and in organizing meetings.

In order to have students undertake a project for *their* own sake, examinations and grades are waived during the Senior Seminar. Instead, those students whose topics prove most worthwhile and interesting for others to hear and see, as determined by the students and the student advisor in each group, are provided time during the final school week to make informal presentations.

All students will submit some written report of their work in the Senior Seminar.

SENIOR SEMINAR GOALS

The goals for the Senior Seminar would include the following:

1. To offset the inevitable senior slump that occurs after college and employment acceptances are assured.
2. To explore new approaches in learning which might prove even more rewarding and meaningful than the traditional classroom pattern.
3. To provide a stimulating learning situation in which students are free to work in an area of a discipline they think is important.
4. To make use of the special talents of the faculty in ways not yet fully realized.
5. To enable students to utilize the entire city as a learning laboratory.
6. To offer students an opportunity to come to grips with at least one aspect of the contemporary world—and with themselves.
7. To enjoy the fun of doing something different.
8. To give students via independent study away from the classroom a taste of college life and adult responsibilities.

OBJECTIONS TO SENIOR SEMINAR

By no means will there be faculty unanimity for the Senior Seminar. "We have not finished all our work," is the most common complaint. "You cannot release students from class for eight weeks and then expect me to prepare them for the final examinations," is another. "Once you have freed the seniors, the juniors will demand the same rights and soon we will have no school at all," may be heard from a traditionally minded school board member. Compromises will have to be made. In schools where final examinations are mandated in June, students may be forced to remain in these classes. But by rearranging schedules so that all such mandated classes meet in the morning or afternoon hours, every student could have a block of time free each day to participate in the Senior Seminar. Other solutions to this problem come easily to mind. Capable students could take the final examination in April or May, based on work already completed. Students could have the option of mastering work on their own that is covered in the classes they no longer attend. Teachers might revise their courses and squeeze out padded content so the class work could be concluded prior to June. All these compromises will necessitate considerable friendly persuasion on the part of the school administrator. But the time and trouble are worth the candle because the Senior Seminar program forces a staff to reexamine priorities. Better still, it offers both students and teachers new learning designs.

Several teachers and not a few students will worry about jumping into a new program for which there were no precedents, no guidelines, no clear understandings of what constitutes success. The absence of grades to force compliance with the few regulations set for the Senior Seminar will also be mentioned as a drawback. "How can we be certain that students will do any work if they are not graded?" a teacher asks. The question reveals worlds about the philosophy of such teachers. And then there are the legal questions. "How do we mark students in our attendance records if they are not present in school for an entire day?" "Should we not wait first for permission from the State Education Department?" "What happens if a student is injured while away from school during the school day?"

A Miller maxim formulated after more than two decades of dealings with the bureaucratic tom-toms is that when attempting new programs, indiscretion is often the better part of valor. An educational experiment that proves successful is always easy to justify later. If a program proves a failure there is then no need for special consideration and a formal waiving of rules. Students who are having an exciting learning experience at the Metropolitan Museum of Art, a ghetto elementary school, a publishing house, or doing research on Arab music are surely as profitably engaged as if they were attending formal school sessions. Indeed, one could claim that this kind of participatory extension education from the school to the community is the better way to insure relevancy in learning.

SENIOR SEMINAR PROJECTS

Simply listing the programs chosen by seniors fails to convey adequately the true sense of excitement and the high degree of interest that is actually aroused. But a listing does indicate the rich variety and the creative nature of their projects. Here are some:

Working with a Narcotics Addict in a Halfway House—A one-to-one relationship between a high school senior and a ten year old.

A Study of Matrices—Three students and a mathematics teacher on a preceptorial plan.

Physical Education in New York City Schools—Visits and interviews and judgments.

Bertrand Russell—An indepth study of the philosopher.

Geometric Painting—Students experimenting in totally new areas of expression.

Zionism—A historical study by student who questioned her parents' bias.

Working at the School for the Deaf—Several students gained new understandings here—one made it her career.

Relationships between Painting and Poetry—Research as well as practical application.

Lessons of the Oppenheimer Case—Extensive work in the city reference center.

Behind the Scenes at the American Museum of Natural History—Meeting the strangest artifacts, people, and learning how values are determined.

Some Thoughts on Pope John—By a devout Catholic who found reason to reaffirm her faith.

A Study of Art Communities—A "way-out" study.

Working with an NBC Television News Crew—A thoroughly exciting experience including some sober thinking on what constitutes news.

The Ecology of the Seashore—Several students found many living forces in "dead" sand and shore.

Report on Parapsychology—Undertaken by student with assistance from college psychologist.

Astronomy Projects at Hayden Planetarium—Planetarium personnel were happy to have students around.

Photographic Exhibition of Communities Along Lexington Avenue Subway Stations—From Wall Street to Harlem, photographs that spoke strikingly about luxury and poverty, beauty and filth along a subway line of the city.

Working in the City Morgue—Nearly a dozen students made blood analyses and learned other aspects of life and death.

"Up in Central Park"—A film made by students of how difficult it is for young people to express their true feelings.

Embryological Development and Experiment with Dyes at Rockefeller Institute—One of the students injected an egg incorrectly and in the process made a discovery about dyes that was unknown to the scientist.

Drama—"Mean to Be Free"—Produced, costumed, directed, arranged by seminar students using seventh grade students as cast members and presented to community groups.

Coats: From Textile to Finished Produce to Store—By a student who thereby learned her father's business.

Proteolytic Enzyme Systems in Developing Rat Tissues—An experiment in treating animals at Francis Delafield Hospital.

Extra Sensory Perception—A well-documented report on the subject.

Testing for Narcotics—Work done at the Laboratory for Addictive Drugs where testing is performed on urine of drug addicts.

"Billy Mitchell Learns to Fly"—A short story written for eleven- and twelve-year-old children.

Black Power—An indepth report by two students—one black, one white, on the power, the promise, and the perils of the new movement.

Proofreading a Dictionary—The following summary submitted by the student:

I was interviewed by a publisher who suggested I read the

manuscript of a new dictionary and see how it was put together. Seminar brought me the promise of a job for the summer proofreading at $3.00 an hour, plus an opportunity to learn editing. It opened up a new field for future thought—a surprisingly new direction. Most important I think, Seminar threw me into contact with people or that class of people I had admired—the sophisticated young college graduates, well-educated men and women. I discovered I could reject a good deal of that world, keep some of my own Brooklynese and be content to fit in neither . . . Like everything else at Hunter, Seminar was a learning experience. It wasn't always pleasant but Seminar stretches your thoughts.

SENIOR SEMINAR PROCEDURES

Prior to the start of the Senior Seminar, the parents should be asked to sign a statement giving their approval to have their child away from school three days each week. In addition, each supervisor at a community agency where the students express a desire to work should be asked to submit a letter indicating his willingness to accommodate the student. He is also requested to sign a special attendance sheet which the student deposits with the school secretary once each week. Teachers can place an "E" for educational trip in the attendance book next to the name of each student who is enrolled in the Seminar and is away from school. And teachers whose regular classes are cancelled by the Senior Seminar are now free to visit students at work in the community agencies. Students and teachers can be placed on their honor to follow these procedures. Rates of absence and tardiness will prove to be considerably below regular school percentages.

Senior Seminars can have a dramatic impact on students, teachers and the community. Students recognize that they are in a school where something different, something new and exciting is happening. Willingly, the school administration will be breaking traditional patterns of school policy. The psychological advantages in creating a positive school climate are tremendous for students when adults respond to their plea that education reflect contemporary interests and needs. By the very nature of the organization and philosophy of the Senior Seminar, students and faculty are encouraged to replace lockstep thinking with new insights, and with new approaches to creative activities. For the community at large, the direct involvement of the school in the life of the city provides innumerable avenues for better understanding and support of the educational program.

On the first official day of the Senior Seminar all the students might attend a special orientation session. "Today we begin a remarkable education experiment," the students would be informed. "After more than a decade of don'ts, of restraints and restrictions, test marks and report cards, courses and credits, you have been 'liberated.' For the next two months you will be bound no more by the grade whip or the attendance stick. No more will you be forced to master material other people think is important. Now you are the judge, you decide what is important, you make the decisions."

Why students have to wait until the last two months of their school life before being allowed to exercise such responsibilities is a question that should be asked—and answered. As we shall see, the Senior Seminar format can serve as a pace setter for greater student initiative in the total curriculum.

In launching a Senior Seminar students must be made fully aware that the success or failure of the experiment will depend primarily on their own efforts. The exact pattern of the program must be clearly delineated and the expectations of the faculty for the students fully stated. Here is one procedure:

> What will happen in the next two months? We have plenty of Cassandras who predict that high school students will mistake liberty for license. A doubting dean at one of our neighboring colleges believes that even undergraduates are too immature for the degree of freedom we propose in this program.
>
> Perhaps the "lookers with alarm" are correct. Perhaps providing what they label "free-floating study" is too rash an experiment for high school students. But we recall another educator who kept the following statement on his desk at Harvard University and acted accordingly: "Behold the turtle; it only makes progress when it is willing to stick its neck out."
>
> Your faculty has elected to stick its neck out. We believe that progress will occur when knowledge is personally meaningful, when education is a living as well as a learning experience. We

think and hope that the Senior Seminar will prove to be such an experience.

Twice each week teachers who have been freed from regular classes will meet in seminar sessions with you. They come as guides, not as goads. The initiative, the inspiration, the design and the finshed product of your work during this period will be your own creation. You are limited only by the bounds of propriety, and by your will to achieve a personal breakthrough on the fringes of your knowledge.

THE TWENTIETH CENTURY FOCUS

"Focus on the Twentieth Century" is one formal title that could be given to the Senior Seminar. To focus on our century makes sense for several reasons. Students feel that they are involved in a time sequence that is directly relevant to their own lives. Furthermore, as can be seen in the list of specific projects, using the present period offers a wide spectrum of imaginative study choices. Finally, in many ways, the twentieth century is least understood and studied by both faculty and students. Although both groups are twentieth century products, our frames of reference are vastly different. To students, Eisenhower, Churchill, and Stalin are names in history textbooks; to most teachers, these men were part of their lives. Students should be made aware of the similarities and differences between the world of today and the period 1900-1960. For example:

Millions of people are alive today who recall what it meant to live at the very beginning of the twentieth century in 1900. Then it was a question of whether we would assume the white man's burden, whether we would keep the Philippines, Guam, and Puerto Rico, and keep our troops in Cuba. Theodore Roosevelt was kicked into the vice presidency because he threatened the fiefdoms of vice and corruption so carefully controlled by the New York power elite. Drug addiction and sexual aberrations are not a discovery of the 1970s.

Then, as now, the madness for money motivated many otherwise decent human beings. Darwin's discoveries about the survival of the fittest in nature were applied ruthlessly to man. Sinclair Lewis describes the cult of capitalism when he introduces Babbitt:

His name was George F. Babbitt. He was forty-six years old now,

in April, 1920, and he made nothing in particular, neither butter
nor shoes nor poetry, but he was nimble in the calling of selling
houses for more than people could afford to pay.[1]

What Toynbee has called the "one damn fact after another"
approach to knowledge is not the goal of a Senior Seminar.
Students should examine the changes in painting, architecture,
music and technology, as they study the life styles of people. They
need to move from the descriptive to the analytical, to ask why
the twentieth century has changed so radically in some ways, so
little in others. What does it mean to be an American in the
twentieth century? How do you define the American spirit, the
American mind, the American creed, the American way? Can
these terms, these generalizations be made with any true sense of
reliability? Margaret Mead points out that mobility and change are
natural by-products of American life which is geared to success
rather than to status.[2] Americans change, she maintains, because
we measure our worth by the distance we have progressed from
our point of departure, rather than the position we now occupy.
Americans are reputed to be competitive, materialistic, and profli-
gate. Our history in the twentieth century is overflowing with
examples of competition, materialism, and profligacy. Critics say
that Americans often do not know what they really want, but
they feel sure they don't have it. America is also composed of the
largest proportion of middle class population in the world. To
what extent are the characteristics of competition, materialism,
and profligacy indigenous American traits; to what extent are they
characteristic middle class traits; to what extent are they universal
characteristics?

Nor should students explore aspects of man in the twentieth
century without considering man's nature. One stimulating learning procedure is to have students immerse themselves in the
philosophy of a particular school and then argue from this
position. For example, several students become "disciples" of

---

[1] Sinclair Lewis, *Babbitt* (New York: Random House Modern Library Edition, 1942),
p. 2.

[2] Margaret Mead, *And Keep Your Powder Dry* (New York: William Morrow and Co.
1949), p. 93. ". . . in America, with the rapid rate of change, most parents know that
the child will not do what the parent did, but something different . . . He must applaud
in his son something which he did not do himself, and something which he has no way
of judging."

orthodox theologians who consider man to be made in the image of God and endowed with an immortal soul. Others become Marxists and regard man primarily in terms of economics. Still others are Freudians and insist that man is propelled by sexual desires and frustrations. Jeffersonians emphasize man's ability to think and act intelligently on the basis of equality with other men. Calvinists maintain that man is born sinful but achieves salvation through God's grace. Romanticists argue that man is born innocent but is corrupted by society. Send students out on independent study programs to research their respective positions and the ensuing debate that occurs when they return will sharpen everyone's thinking.

Senior Seminars offer unique opportunities for students to ask and answer questions which unfortunately are not found in the regular curriculum—questions such as: What is success? What is happiness? How are they achieved? Why do these concepts differ with national groups? Glib generalizations must be identified. Attributing national traits to a people bound by the same government or the same location can reach limits of absurdity. Oscar Wilde had a fine time speculating whether the fogs caused the English mentality or the English mentality caused the fogs. Some scholars have repudiated the whole idea of a national character and insist that the national character was invented by historians. It would seem entirely plausible that when rural people work by themselves, and are largely responsible to themselves, accommodating their routine to the rhythm of the season, they will develop different traits from urban people who work for others, are bunched together in cities, and have their lives regulated by clocks. "Buy now, pay later" has in our century replaced the ancient homily in Poor Richard's Almanac, "A penny saved is a penny earned." Gone, too, is Franklin's cheerful couplet, "Early to bed, and early to rise, makes a man healthy, wealthy and wise." Most people on our planet go to bed early and they are up at sunrise but they are sick, poor, and uneducated. Solutions that may fit a nation with rich soil, a stable government, and room for expansion cannot be exported to other lands and other people. However students choose to develop their Senior Seminar, their frame of reference as to the nature of man in the twentieth century will have to be selective, and is certain to be in conflict with other hypotheses. An exciting prospect!

THE PAST AS PRELUDE

Young people today are told by some modern soothsayers that they no longer need to be concerned with the past. "You are born into a scientific age, an age in which the word 'impossible' means 'maybe not tomorrow, but soon,' " they hear. Ninety percent of all scientists who ever lived on this earth are alive and making a contribution today. And the litany for science is droned into the minds of youth:

> Science has cured disease, conquered space, lengthened life. Science has devised satellites to accelerate communication, predict the weather, and provide instant coverage of coronations and killings. Science has automated factories, computerized the laws of supply and demand, given us more leisure time, the supersonic plane, and population control.

The Senior Seminar students should not be asked is airplane travel better, but do we have better people traveling? The question is not solely whether work is automated and effortless but whether people see purpose and pride in what they are doing. The question to be asked is what actually happens to humans in a scientific world when computers and technology can develop interchangeable jobs and interchangeable people?

For students who will continue to live in the second half of the twentieth century and into the twenty-first, one thing is certain— the boundary lines in human terms between what is true and what is false, between right and wrong, will become more blurred, more difficult to determine. Choices will still have to be made, for in a society where there are no value priorities and no links to the past, there is no future. What we love and how we love may change but the *need* for love will continue. Styles may change but the *question* of style will continue. Values may change but the need to have some standard of judgment will continue. Scientific inquiry can advance man in understanding his nature. The danger is that in the process man will be redefined into an energy system,—a thing to be manipulated and dissected. We have not even begun to grapple with the ominous nature of a scientific world in which the genetic code has been broken and scientists are able to produce custom-made men or women according to the needs of the national interest. When that day arrives, humanity will indeed become a tool, a mechanism of the State.

The Senior Seminar program allows students to deal directly with these issues. They will also deal with the phoniness of life in their search for identity and truth—the everyman themes. They will have options. How they face these options and how they search for answers become their twentieth century discoveries in the Senior Seminar. And in the process they may discover themselves.

SENIOR SEMINAR EVALUATION

How does one evaluate the Senior Seminar? How can we prove that it is worthwhile? Alas, theory and practice do not always run in parallel lines. An old cartoon shows two teachers discussing their teaching techniques. "I teach children to be insightful," says the first teacher. "I teach them to develop their creative personalities," says the other. And a student who has classes with both teachers remarks, "I hate school." For a variety of reasons some students and some teachers will choose not to follow the Senior Seminar procedures. A few students may insist that the Senior Seminar still includes a basic distrust of students because attendance records must still be kept. "You are not treating us as adults," they complain. "If you really had faith in us you would not impose compulsory attendance requirements." For such radical thinking, the reasoned explanation of legal restrictions and responsibilities will not be heard. School administrators who cannot or will not follow a total laissez-faire policy have no recourse but to insist on the minimum operational framework of the Senior Seminar. Given a fresh taste of freedom, several students will be unable to resist the temptation to substitute license for liberty. A few students have such deep-seated home and personal problems that nothing in the Senior Seminar, even when they make their own choices, seems relevant. Such students need professional counseling rather than new schooling approaches. Nor will negative reaction come exclusively from students. Teachers who have been educated to control a classroom, to assert their authority, may find an open school environment too hot to handle. When the grade threat is abolished and the other classic restraints on students are removed, some teachers will be at an absolute loss to function. Others may move to the opposite extreme and accept any lackluster work done by students as an important expression of style, feeling or involvement. We have here a serious indictment of our school system. Far too little effort has been expended in teaching the students and the staff how to cope with freedom in a meaningful way.

To maintain, therefore, that the Senior Seminar will be an unqualified success, that all the eight goals listed above will be realized, or that all the students will launch into their projects with zest and purpose, would be an outrageous lie. No matter what the incentives, some students can be expected to waste their free periods. When the usual school restraints on freedom of action are removed, they possess insufficient drive or desire to work on their own. These students use the days away from school to sleep late, or to latch on to a good paying job prior to the summer rush for work from students in other schools.

Other problems will arise when a Senior Seminar is offered. Goodwill on the part of the humanities faculty and the administration may not be accepted by all students. In several instances teachers have found it inexpedient or unrewarding to hold weekly tutorial sessions with uncooperative students. Our enthusiasm and high expectations too often cause us to forget Emerson's warning that the greatest need in life is to have someone make us do what we can. In the face of some failures educators are forced to rationalize that by the senior year some students will rebel against any program. "Given a chance," one teacher remarked, "they would even vote against Sunday." A number of students can therefore be expected to do nothing. But doing nothing is a punishment too. When the students who have made valuable use of their free time give glowing reports of their Senior Seminar programs, do-nothing students realize that they have punished themselves in wasting a golden opportunity. And such a lesson may be as valuable as any other goals.

The Senior Seminar is predicated on a positive rather than a negative educational approach. To abandon the Senior Seminar because a small minority of the students and teachers are not committed to or capable of following the rules of the game has little logic. To do so would be to punish an entire class because a few could not be trusted.

No matter what procedure is devised, no matter how much the teachers and students are consulted and involved in the process, some iconoclasts can be expected to disagree and disobey. Rather than spending time demanding total conformity, a wiser course is to believe that the majority of students and teachers who find value in the Senior Seminar format deserve the school's attention and support. In short, the Senior Seminar requires a school to take a chance on the inherent decency and humanity of people. In schools where the freedom provided by the Senior Seminar has been offered, the overwhelming majority of the students, the faculty, and the community have been delighted.

In several schools, an on-going independent evaluation committee of teachers, parents, and students is formed to examine the Senior Seminar's pluses and minuses. To avoid bias, no committee member should be a Senior Seminar participant. Without exception, students and teachers in Senior Seminars claim they have gained more than would have occurred in the traditional program. Most students insist they experienced no sense of loss in not completing their regular classes through the final month of school.

An excerpt from one student's evaluation sheet summarizes the feelings of many who spent time both in school and on the project:

> For me the Senior Seminar was a success. I never felt depressed to come to school during this period because I sensed that each day would be new and exciting and it was. I believe I worked hard, learned much, and never felt pressured. I have never felt so free and content. There are enough problems trying to cope with one's self and others without making formal school education a painful experience, something which I did not encounter during the program.

Here is a comment from a student who worked in a slum:

> Everyone comments on how bad the neighborhood is and tells me to be careful. I've said the same thing to others, but can I work with these people if I am afraid of them? ... As I went home, all I could think of was that I was beginning to see that these people are really people, with hopes and dreams similar to those of people living in the "better" parts of the city. I begin to think of them more as my people. This is a big step, perhaps the biggest I will make in the project.

In each successive year of the Senior Seminar, more attention should be paid to helping students develop projects before the program actually begins. Students will build on the experiences of students in previous projects. In its second year, Senior Seminar students can be expected to dream large dreams. Eleven seniors in the German language class of one school scrounged sufficient funds to go with their German-born teacher on a three week educational adventure in West Germany. In another school one student invented a simulation game for seventh grade students studying international relations. Nearly a dozen students in a large city received the cooperation of a publishing house and attempted to produce a sophisticated magazine for high school students. The venture failed but both students and teachers felt that the experience was worth the effort. Several students in a Senior Seminar were accepted as laboratory assistants at the New York City Medical Examiner's office and several more helped the city hall staff handle telephoned citizen complaints.

Once the Senior Seminar is generally accepted, a more radical approach to changing the entire senior year curriculum should be anticipated from a school's more articulate students and teachers. For example:

> The Senior Seminar is fine as far as it goes, but May is far away. Why wait until we are all fed up with school to offer your package of goodies?

> The new program is too abrupt a break with all the prior learning we have given students. If the Senior Seminar has educational merit, should we not see if we can relate the education in our classrooms from September to May with the education the students receive outside the school in May and June? Why not make the whole year a Senior Seminar?

> Must we be controlled by the bell instead of by the nature of each lesson? Just when we get into a really profound discussion in the Senior Seminar the bell rings and we have to wait 24 hours or longer to start again.

> Why not move to independent study for the entire senior year and let us have more that a two month nibble at being on our own?

> Let's develop a truly integrated curriculum in the humanities.

These questions and suggestions will sound most appetizing to those on the faculty and in the community who are eager to seize the opportunity for more thoroughgoing curriculum reform than is provided by the May through June Senior Seminar. The successes as well as the limitations of the Senior Seminar thus can become a springboard for advancing to a year-round multidisciplinary humanities curriculum.

CHAPTER 5

Organizing a Humanities Curriculum
–Phase One

QUESTIONS TO ASK

A humanities curriculum should begin with an idea, with hope, and with many questions. We know that most high school students already have more knowledge than they know what to do with. Instead of continuing to cram more material into autonomous courses, can we offer some sense of synthesis, with more accent on meaning than memorization? Can we redirect the school curriculum to echo the way life is actually seen, heard, and lived outside school? Can the school play a role beyond subject mastery in improving the life style of its community? Can the present structure of separated, segmented subjects be viewed instead as a totality? Can we, to use that much-abused word again, make education relevant—revelant to the needs and interests of the school's clients, its students? At the same time can we offer students more options, more freedom of choice, and can we expect more commitment because they have made a choice? Can we stop doing to and for students and begin to do *with* students? Dare we deal with questions which are not already answered in the back of the book or in the teacher's head?

Other tough questions need to be asked. Would teachers from different disciplines be willing to work together, would teachers be able to see further than their own subject box, would teachers be ready to move into a circle of students and serve as a resource and a listener rather than primarily as a judge? Could a teacher be a person of authority without being authoritarian? Could we unshackle the prison of the school clock which regulates class time? Could the length of each class and the size of each group be determined not by administrative convenience but on whether it helped students learn? Could we even leave the school to learn, could we radically change the student-teacher relationship patterns, could we expect students would want to learn if there were no threats like grades, detention halls, or suspension to compel conformity for an entire school year?

A humanities curriculum should begin with an idea; it should also begin with an infusion of some funds. In the best of all possible worlds, or in heaven, money would not be needed to bring teachers together during the summer months to reorganize the school curriculum. Neither of these places resembles the real world of public elementary and secondary schools. President Kennedy's inaugural exhortation to "Ask not what your country can do for you, ask what you can do for your country" has not made noticeable headway with business, industry, labor, governmental employees, or the professions. Despite rumors to the contrary, teachers are not immune from paying rent, eating, and making other purchases. Extra work deserves, indeed requires, extra remuneration.

Devising a new curriculum during the school year after each school day is over is asking teachers to assume an extremely exhausting assignment. Few people outside of the teaching fraternity really comprehend how enervating life can be after working with eager young minds and bodies from 8:30 A.M. to 3:00 P.M. five days each week. Most teachers are too tired in the late afternoon to develop creative plans. Tempers are raw, nerves are brittle, and the desire to leave the school building is often overwhelming. For similar reasons faculty meetings held in the late afternoons after the close of school are usually considered an intrusion rather than a stimulant. A hoary teacher anecdote relates to late afternoon faculty meetings. "When I die," a veteran teacher comments, "I hope it will be at a faculty meeting because the transition between life and death will be hardly noticeable." The story may be apocryphal but the theme is true. A humanities curriculum, indeed any new program that requires considerable concentration and reflection, should be organized initially during the summer when minds are clear from routine tasks. If summer pay is non-existent, then teachers must be given released time during the school year to develop their plans for a humanities curriculum.

Seed time and seed money for planning are needed. And if the humanities proposal is sound, and you are fortunate, funds and time may be forthcoming. Sometimes the local school system, sometimes the State Education Department or the U.S. Office of Education, sometimes private foundations will provide the initial wherewithal. At Hunter we asked the National Endowment for the Arts and the Humanities in Washington, D.C. for assistance. In our first proposal, the humanities curriculum was conceived as a two-year high school program embracing the eleventh and twelfth years. In the covering letter to the National Endowment for the Arts and the Humanities appeared this statement:

> We have no intention of submitting our humanities curriculum to an apathetic or uninformed faculty. Our design will aim for commitment and direct involvement on the part of the majority of the staff.[1]

So it was written. But it is well known that the streets of hell are paved with good intentions. Out of innocence, or arrogance, I neglected to have the faculty first vote on whether a humanities program should even be considered. Well known was that the primary requirement existed for a restructuring of the curriculum—teachers who were both competent and compassionate and willing to experiment. Well known, too, was that the students were eager for change. And it was equally well known that without funds to undertake the detailed work over the summer, and to pay for time freed to meet, plan, and evaluate so elaborate a program during the academic year, a humanities curriculum

---

[1]Letter to Mrs. Joan Smith, National Foundation on the Arts and the Humanities, 1800 G Street, N.W., Washington, D.C., 20506, April 28, 1967.

debate would be only another frustrating and futile academic exercise. "Why raise false hopes for a dream that most likely would come to naught?" I decided. On the basis of such logic,—or illogic, the initial proposal was sent to Washington, D.C. without prior full staff consultation and approval.

But administrator's motives are always suspect. Several teachers felt that the dice had been loaded by first applying for funds. "You make it difficult to examine objectively the question of the merits of a humanities curriculum when the possibility of receiving funds is in the offing," protested some of the staff. Looking back at the incident one would agree that these teachers were probably correct. An administrator is always on a razor's edge in knowing how far to pressure for change. In a democratic nation, the best leaders are those who, when a difficult task is accomplished, will have the community believe that they have done it themselves. When a school official is three steps ahead of the faculty he is considered a leader; when he is ten or more steps ahead, the faculty is chasing him! No fool-proof prescription can possibly be offered for each school situation. Some people are born with this sixth sense of awareness. Such fortunate souls make excellent administrators. Most human beings learn this art through the more bruising process of trial and error. The question of commitment and know-how on change—change that means real educational progress—is a major benchmark that separates the administrative technician from the statesman.

FACULTY PARTICIPATION

The faculty made important changes in the original proposal. A two year humanities curriculum proved unrealistic. We acknowledged that few schools in our country would be willing to "sacrifice" that much time from "established, legitimate" subjects for a humanities curriculum. In the junior year most students have too many solid requirements in social studies, English, physical education, and a major elective area to free the schedule for the humanities.

A senior year humanities curriculum seemed to make more sense. Every high school in the nation, both public and private, must face the consequences of the senior slump—students tired of still more English, more social studies and other subjects taught for the most part in the same way as in the previous years. A new approach to the teaching of the traditional disciplines on the twelfth grade level would have an excellent chance of a welcome reception. By the senior year most of the mandated subjects have been taken. We were aware that many school systems were eager to explore new ideas for the senior year. The Senior Seminar program introduced at Hunter and publicized via the educational media resulted in a barrage of letters from schools asking for guidance in organizing similar formats.

Nevertheless, at Hunter and at other schools, teachers would be most reluctant to part with successful senior year electives already in existence. Senior electives are considered by many faculty to be the desserts of teaching. With the oldest students in school, a teacher has wider latitude to introduce more sophisticated concepts, and in general to work on an adult level. To scrap these elective subjects would guarantee having many teachers take an adverse position toward the humanities. Once again, compromise was necessary. Our solution was to permit students to elect the humanities curriculum for an entire morning or afternoon session and to choose three free electives for the remainder of the school day in their senior year. When scheduling, the student's elective choices in mathematics, science, foreign language, advanced placement classes, etc., would have first priority. And every attempt would be made to have elective choices available for a full morning or afternoon schedule. Thus if a student requests courses in history, French, and physiology which meet during the first three periods of the school day, she is placed in the afternoon humanities curriculum. For some students who give the highest priority to science courses with several laboratory sessions each week, the humanities curriculum would probably not be an option. Other seniors who prefer the traditional program, and students who are accelerated from the tenth to the twelfth grade would be scheduled for regular courses in English and social studies as well as other electives rather than the humanities. In this way senior electives are retained and room is still provided in the schedule for a three credit humanities curriculum.

Students enrolled in the afternoon humanities curriculum for example, could have the following schedule:

Period	Monday	Tuesday	Wednesday	Thursday	Friday
1	— — — — — — — — — —	— — — HI	STORY — —	— — — — — — — —	— — — —
2	— — — — — — — — — —	— — — FR	ENCH — —	— — — — — —	— — —
3	— — — — — — — —	— — PHYS	IOLOGY —	— — — — — —	— — — —
4	— — — — — — —	— — — L	UNCH — — —	— — — — — —	— — — —
5		H U M A N I T I E S W O R K S H O P S			Humanities: Community
6 > 7	Humanities Seminars	Humanities Lecture-Demonstra-tions	Humanities Seminar or Independent Programs	Humanities Seminars	Visits or Group Work

A morning humanities schedule would offer the same flexible structure for periods 1, 2 and 3 that is outlined above for periods 5, 6 and 7. Students in the morning humanities would take other electives in the afternoon periods, perhaps courses in mathemetics, advanced chemistry, and psychology. A student in a morning humanities program would then follow the pattern shown on page 100. In both programs the lunch period can overlap into the humanities curriculum thereby providing still more flexibility.

THE BEGINNING

No guaranteed formula exists for the number of teachers who

Period	Monday	Tuesday	Wednesday	Thursday	Friday
1	H U M A N I T I E S W O R K S H O P S				Humanities: Community Visits or Group Work
2 3	Humanities Seminars	Humanities Lecture-Demonstra-tions	Humanities Seminar or Independent Programs	Humanities Seminars	
4	— — — — — — — — — — — — — L U N C H — — — — — — — — — — — — — — — — —				
5	— — — — — — — — — — M A T H E M A T I C S — — — — — — — — — — — —				
6	— — — — — — — — — — P S Y C H O L O G Y — — — — — — — — — — — —				
7	— — — — — — — A D V A N C E D C H E M I S T R Y — — — — — — — —				

AD. CHEMISTRY

should constitute an effective committee. If an administrator is seeking success, he should begin with volunteers rather than draftees; he should express in deed as well as in word his own personal interest and support of the program. Hunter began with eight teachers, two each in English and social studies and one in music, art, drama, and the dance. All eight volunteered to prepare a detailed blueprint for a twelfth grade multidisciplinary humanities curriculum which would be submitted to the entire staff for their criticisms and approval. The assignment, they discovered, was not a simple one. Although a thematic design was adopted, many months were to elapse before a unity of theme was devised.

What areas in a multidisciplinary twelfth grade humanities curriculum dealing with human values should properly and meaningfully be placed in the program? Everyone can agree that the learning must be exciting, that the students should come to class eagerly rather than dutifully or reluctantly. Observed one teacher, "The eagerness and seriousness with which students communicate to us about their activities outside the classroom must be aroused for their work inside the classroom. Otherwise how can we justify the existence of the humanities curriculum or school itself?"

Agreement must also be made to avoid structuring the humanities curriculum into another public relations show which looks great on paper. Not needed are more educational gimmicks which create fancy mechanistic shifts. They put students through the motions but keep them uninvolved. Nor would a professional faculty be content with a superficial treatment of many humanistic areas. Like the American tourist trip through twelve European countries in seven days, such humanities programs substitute snapshots for understanding.

The committee can be asked to reflect on learning from at least three perspectives:

1. To examine what areas in the present curriculum are not introduced by the senior year and could be integrated in a humanities curriculum—for example, aspects of philosophy, anthropology, sociology, psychology, and studies of Asian and African cultures.

2. To integrate the separate functioning disciplines into more direct, coherent relationships.

3. To radicalize the school schedule by providing more opportunities for independent work, more outside guests, more utilization of the city as the school laboratory, more flexibility in teacher-student contacts.

TEACHER REFERENCE POINTS

Many teachers who have been accustomed to working solely in their own discipline will be reluctant to take on the role of resource person or guide with students in seminar sessions. Such reluctance is understandable. A teacher's traditional role has been that of answer giver. In seminar sessions a book or film may be discussed that the teacher may never have read or seen before. What questions then to ask? What directions might the discussion follow? What ideas should be stressed? To help a teaching staff in this new student-teacher learning environment, the teacher "expert" on the humanities team for each work to be used should be asked to prepare "reference points"—a brief tabulation of suggested readings, quotations, questions, and ideas which will provide the staff with options and perspectives for the seminar sessions.

Here are some examples of "teacher reference points" along with essay questions compiled by a team of Hunter English and social studies teachers including Miriam Burstein, Jane Greenspan, Rosemarie Laster and Richard Peck:

Reference Points for *The Republic* and *The Apology*

SOCRATES' WORLD 470-399 B. C.

His was the world of Pericles, following the Persian Wars. Like all Athenian boys, except slaves, he stayed at home with his mother until he was eight, then was educated by men in reading, writing, arithmetic, "music" (including flute, lyre, singing, dance, poetry and literature) and gymnastics. From eighteen to twenty, he performed military service, then became a citizen, able to vote, run for office and ply his trade of stonemasonry and sculpting.

The Persian Wars had engendered new feelings of unity, new dreams of democracy and equality, new belief in justice in this world, all of which resulted in the limitation of the power of the hereditary oligarchy, the Areopagus. For the first time, the whole Assembly made the laws, the Council of Five Hundred became the sole executive, and paid jurymen in people's law courts judged offenders. But, at the same time, despite Pericles' repeated warnings, Athens was increasingly arrogant abroad, bent on conquest, willing to enslave others, even other Greeks.

Population is estimated at a little over 400,000, but of these only about 42,000 were free male citizens. The Attic language and coinage were becoming dominant, Athens assumed leadership in trade, and was becoming a middle class society more and more interested in moneymaking for its own sake.

Socrates was molded as a boy by Herodotus' view of

Athens as the noble home of the Parthenon where all men could approach the gods, where Homer and Hesiod pointed the way to heroism and glory. He read Sophocles and saw fate and justice at odds. He learned from the lyric poet Simonides both the ennobling and the marketplace aspects of polis ethics.

As a teenager, he experienced the democratic revolution of the Periclean advent. He lived and fought through imperialist conquest, rebellion, siege and plague. He was in his sixties when Spartan victors pulled down the Long Walls which guarded Athens and the Hellenic world began to crumble.

He was a believer in Hesiod's *eris*—that healthy competition that makes for improved performance—and applied it to the intellectual competition which he believed would lead to truth. He came to believe that he had a divine mission on earth to test the truth of all things. He espoused poverty (as well as a shrew) unlike the Sophists who would only argue for fees.

Socrates wrote nothing. Most of what we know of his dialogues come from Plato. Two, *The Republic* and *The Laws,* are didactic in the sense that they prescribe answers; the others pose open-ended questions.

With *The Apology,* written about three years after Socrates' death, scholars have been more content to give Socrates credit for this dialogue and see Plato more as history's tape recorder of those final days. Socrates did, after all, die for what he believed and presumably knew what he believed.

A word about two major themes in Hellenic aspirations. One is belief in *the world of forms.* There was, to them, an ideal *anything*—the perfect robe, the perfect pillar, perfect truth, beauty, justice—created in the minds of the gods, glimmering somewhere out in the universe, never fully perceived by man, but forever to be emulated. An act, an object, a thought or feeling, had *virtu,* was good, to the extent that it approached the divine form. These forms were seen as absolute, unchanging, eternal. Socrates can ask, "What is the just man?" or "What is the just state?" because he *knows* that there is one immutable standard of justice.

The second theme is the Hellenic conception of the individual as the-citizen-of-the-polis, one and inseparable. In Greek, *hoi polloi,* "the men," equals "the citizens of the polis." While Greek history is littered with the bodies of individuals who came into conflict with the polis (and Socrates is only one of these), the goal was for total compatibility between the state and its microcosm, man. This ideal explains Socrates' credibility to his listeners when he postulates his structured republic in which each man, frozen to his job and status, happily does "his own thing" for the good of the state.

THE REPUBLIC

Its structure roughly looks like this:

Book I and the first half of Book II, to the paragraph beginning, "I had long admired the genius of Glaucon and Adeimantus," asks, "What is the just man?"

Book II (second half), Book III, Book IV
Constructs the "first state" as the place to look for justice; describes the classification of people into gold, silver, brass, and iron, the education of the guardians, the institution of censorship, economic and population controls, the state's prosperity as each man minds his business.

Books V, VI, VII
Construction of the "second state" in which each member of the polis belongs to everyone else; equality of women, communality of children, the end of enslavement of other Greeks, rule by the philosopher-kings; the analogy of the cave as the key to the role of the philosopher-king.

Books VIII, IX
Perversions of state and man; the search for pleasure as opposed to true happiness; tyranny as the supremacy of pleasure-seeking.

Book X
The harmony among philosophy, music and poetry, the achievement of happiness in this world and the next.

The scene of *The Republic* follows the festival of Bendis (a goddess imported from Thrace). Polymarchus runs after Socrates and the others to invite them for dinner at his father's home, and offers as bait the promise of an equestrian torchlight race. The dialogue continues among Socrates, Polymarchus, Glaucon, Adeimantus and Cleitophon. Cephalus appears only briefly at the beginning and Thrasymachus subsides into silence after his big scene.

Some Avenues of Questioning on Book I and the First Half of Book II:

What do we know about Socrates and his life-work from the dialogue form? What reservations, if any, do you have about the form? Why?

Compare Cephalus' view of old age with your own. How would you explain differences? If you were a Greek, how might you try to justify your admiration of the wisdom of the elderly? How relevant is the experience of your parents to you? If you feel it isn't, why isn't it?

Do Simonides' descriptions of the just man tell us anything about Greek society? About American business ethics? How would you account for similarities or differences? If Socrates' definition of the just man sounds familiar to you, where have you heard it before?

Do you agree with Thrasymachus that the strong impose their will upon the weak and then call it justice? Reasons for your answer? Who in America today might make out the same argument? Would they be right? Does the leader lead just because he has the power? Is law just the tool of the power structure? Should you obey law imposed by someone stronger than you? Is consent, even in a democracy, just a fiction?

Why was it so easy for the Greeks to assume that there *is* such a thing as justice? Are we so sure that there is one unswerving standard of justice? If not, why not? If you had to qualify an act as just or unjust, what criteria would you use?

Questions: Book VI

Who *is* Plato's philosopher? Would you want to be "the spectator of all time and all existence"? Why or why not?

Would you agree with Glaucon that the philosopher-king could easily be the worst of men? Reasons? And what about his other argument that no one will pay any attention to the philosopher? Who in fiction or in real life would you say approaches being a philosopher-king? Why did you choose this person? Can someone be both a philosopher-king and an effective leader at the same time? Would people of other times and other societies have come to the same conclusion· that you did? Why or why not?

If you were trying to ascend to the utmost reaches of your capabilities, what "gymnastics of the soul" would you prescribe for yourself? Socrates talks about the "natural unity of ideas." Have you ever felt this perception yourself?

When? How did it make you feel?

Why do we tend to want our leaders to be nobler, more honest and wiser than we are? *Can* they be better than the society which produced them? If they seem to be, how would you explain it? What do you think the personal price of leadership might be? Rewards? Why would Martin Luther King or Robert Kennedy go on despite threats on their lives?

Questions: Book VII

Whom do you think Socrates had in mind as the unchainer of the first man on the bench? How might you have felt if you were the one unchained? Would you agree that such a release would always have to come from someone else? Why or why not?

What happens to the individual unchained as he finds his way towards the mouth of the cave? How does he feel about what's happening? How would *you* feel if your whole experience of reality were cut out from under you? What might keep you going?

Why can't our cave-dweller look at the sun (the ultimate good) immediately? Do you think it's true that for many higher perceptions there must be intermediate growth experiences? Can you recall any in your own life? What might be some of the temptations to stay alone in the light and never return to the cave? Why, according to Socrates, *must* he return? Do you think for *you* commitment to *your* personal truth and fulfillment is enough? *Should* it be enough?

What does the man in the light experience on the way back to the darkness of the cave? How credible is he to the people still chained to the bench? How can he make himself more credible, so that the others will let themselves be freed? *Should* he unchain them against their will? By what right? Does he have the right *not* to unchain them? Can you remember occasions when you have resisted things done "for your own good"?

Socrates felt that his life was a mission to seek truth that came from the gods. Could *you* find a life commitment that came from this or some other source? Would you want to have such a commitment? What might it cost you? What might be its rewards? Where would you look for it first—in yourself or in the needs of others? Would it make a difference where you started?

Do you believe that each person can be a lover of truth and wisdom? If so, to what extent? If not, what limitations do you see?

THE APOLOGY

The action occurs in 399 B.C., four years after Athens has thrown out the bloody Thirty, the occupation government of Sparta after her victory in the Peloponnesian War. The democratic constitution has been restored, but Athens is anxious to find scapegoats for her defeat. Socrates, 70, has been accused by three men, Meletus, Anytus and Lycon, of corrupting the youth and of impiety. His case comes before a citizen court of 500 jurors. A majority may convict.

The Apology is three speeches. In the first, Socrates refutes both the formal charges and other slanderous stories circulated about him, justifies his life and beliefs, and exposes Meletus' insincerity. The court finds him guilty, by a majority of 60 votes, and the accusers demand the death penalty. In his second speech, Socrates proposes that instead of punishment he receive the distinguished citizen's award, public financial support, or, at worst, pay a moderate fine of about $600.00. The court votes for death. In the final speech, Socrates calmly accepts the decision and says farewell.

Questions: Speech I

How does Socrates explain the enmity and malice of others toward him? Can you remember the last time someone made you feel foolish or stupid? How did you feel toward that person? Suppose that same person said to you, "I know I know nothing." Would you like him more or less?

How does Socrates defend his life and work as divinely inspired? By Greek standards of proof, did he make out a convincing case? By your standards?

Why, though offered the chance to live if he stops being a gadfly, does he refuse? Who else can you think of that's made the same choice? The opposite choice? What arguments did these others use to defend their position? What do you think of the merits of each of these?

When he warns the court that if they kill him they'll be injuring themselves more than they injure him, what does he mean? Was he right? Do leaders really care about history's verdict? Should they?

Is passive acceptance of evil as bad as active performance of it? Does the Eichmann argument that "We only followed orders" fully convince you that there is no complicity?

Questions: Speech II

Explain his argument that he deserves honor and public support rather than punishment. Do you agree with him? If you were a member of the court, how might you have reacted?

Why do you think he put the court on the spot by ruling out other choices of punishment, like imprisonment or exile? Do you think it was his idea to accept a fine? If not his, whose? Why the suggestion?

How can he say that he's not afraid of death? Was he convincing? Do you think life is to be preserved, no matter what?

Questions: Speech III

Why does Socrates refuse to plead for his life? How do you think the court might have reacted to his refusal to do so? Suppose he had, and was freed for a few more years in which important work was accomplished. Would his pleas have been worthwhile? Does martyrdom always achieve its goals?

Does Socrates, in his attitude toward his accusers, actually *live* and *be* the "just man" he idealized in *The Republic?* Why or why not?

Could his final statements about death and the future of his sons be viewed as summaries of his whole life? In what ways? Do you think your parents' last thoughts would be about you? Would yours be about them?

What evidence that his work would go on might have comforted Socrates?

Have you been thinking, during this discussion, what might I be willing to die for? If not, why not? If you can't conceive of dying for anything, could you ask, "What would I be willing to *live* for?"

Throughout the discussions above, I have often asked, "Do you agree. . . ?" or "Would you want to be. . . ?" rather than "Why does he say that. . . ?", which would contain a built-in summary or conclusion. I have assumed that students will be required to supply reasons for their conclusions. I have also assumed that students who take a position will be asked to argue against themselves.

KING LEAR

There are all too many questions posed by *King Lear* (as is revealed by even a cursory look at the *King Lear Perplex,*[2] hereafter referred to as *P.*), and we might as well acknowledge this from the start. In this work, more than any other we plan to read this year, we must stick to the principle that we are raising questions rather than answering them, and if we can lead our students to a sense of awe about the enormity of the play's problems, we will be doing a good job.

Although each student will reach a different level of understanding, there are certain common experiences we ought to be able to draw upon. All will have read *Hamlet* and *Macbeth* and will have, we hope, a reasonable facility in following Shakespearian language and dramatic structure. But if they are familiar with these other dramas, they should also be quick to see that *Lear* is more tremendous—more sweepingly tragic, perhaps, especially as it occurs in no definable time or place. Its source is more ancient, less relevant to history than are the other plays, and in this sense it seems closer to such a work as *Oedipus Rex,* which we intend to compare it to in our opening session. They will have read Sophocles' Oedipus plays recently, and we hope the intensity and power of the Stravinsky music will serve as a reminder of the terror and enormity of great mythic tradition.

Any discussion of Lear tends to feature such hyperbole as I see myself using—words like terror and enormity. Charles Lamb's famous comment (*P.* 15) that the play is "unactable" means that it transcends acting rather than that it is a bad play; as he says, the play is "Beyond all art" and is "a Leviathan." Another piece of melodramatic language is Edith Sitwell's (*P.* 117) who even makes a neat parallel with Oedipus. An excellent summarizing statement is Swinburne's (*P.* 39).

---

[2]Helmut Bonheim, ed., *The King Lear rerplex* (Belmont, California: Wadsworth Publishing, 1960).

First of all, the play must be in effect translated, scene by scene, with as much reading aloud of passages as there is time for. Although we want to go on into the matters of theme and impact, this is primarily a piece of poetry and a drama, and we should make sure that students understand what is happening and the magical effectiveness of even short passages ("ripeness is all" for instance) in terms of language. For teachers uncertain about any scenes, I would recommend the complete plot summary in *Reader's Encyclopedia of Shakespeare*[3] of Campbell and Quinn, but any review book version of the play will do.

This appreciation of the language is especially important since the action of the play is full of implausibilities, of unlikely behavior on the part of almost everybody, and students will expect this to be explained or at least dealt with, but to begin with we have to admit it is there. (If the students don't pose such questions, we should.) For instance, why does Lear announce that he will divide his kingdom according to his daughters' answers when it is otherwise indicated that he has already decided on the division? Bradley answers this (*P.* 43) referring to Coleridge (*P.* 16).

The *Perplex* is only a selection of what has been said, and since its publication, other significant commentary has come out, notably the work of the Pole Jan Kott *(Shakespeare Our Contemporary,* a Doubleday Anchor paperback) who has been much admired by the Royal Shakespeare Company and Joseph Papp and his staff. Kott says that Lear is an early example of the Theater of the Absurd, but he cites the ideas of earlier critics, notably G. Wilson Knight (in *P.* 146). Another such view of Lear in *P.* (p. 138) is by psychiatrist Arpaud Paunez.

But how much use can we, as teachers in this course, make of the *Perplex*? It is not an explanation of the play; if anything, it serves to confuse. It has a useful topical index, but the citations for any topic are by design inconsistent or at least varied. As a casebook it can be used by students on any level, who may come up with different answers to a given problem. Furthermore each entry really demands further investigation of the background and attitudes of the entry's

---

[3]O.J. Campbell and E.G. Quinn, editors, *Reader's Enclyclopedia of Shakespeare* (New York: T.Y. Crowell, 1966).

author. For us to study the book in preparation for this course would be something like sinking into quicksand, unless the nature of the book is carefully kept in mind. I would hope that some of our students could make fruitful use of the book for independent study, but again with some direction and instruction about the authors quoted.

Here are some entries that might help with the questions that are likely to come up. First of all, the details of the plot have occasioned many carping comments. Tolstoy's crotchety animadversions (*P.* 50) strike me as sounding like certain school girls. His facts are correct, but his *tone* as he lists the implausibilities of the plot is so offensive that he clearly deserves the answer given by George Orwell (*P.* 85) even though it constitutes an *ad hominem* attack on Tolstoy. Orwell is often cited in schools and colleges for the lucidity of his thinking and his writing, and this passage seems to me to be eminently calm and reasoned. This digression of mine, about Orwell, only substantiates what I suggested above about the ever-widening circles of commentary possible. Another clear presentation of the objection to the plot commonly offered may be found in A.C. Bradley (*P.* 43).

The largest plot problem is the fact that Lear and Cordelia die at the end. We must deal with this even though it involves the normally peripheral scholarly questions of how Shakespeare adapts his source material, and how his text has been changed since his death. These subjects are important but not primary in reference to all his plays; in *Lear* it seems an essential part of even an elementary study.

The death of the two wronged protagonists has led to the common view that the play is, in Oscar Campbell's words, "one of the most terrible expressions of pessimism in all literature," but, as Cambell continues, others take the play "to be a message of hope and faith—an exalted, half-Christian, half-Stoic morality play, a profound commentary on life set against a backdrop of eternity." Campbell expounds further (*P.* 108) on the meaning of the terms Christian and Stoic, which come up often in Lear criticism, as they do, of course, in our humanities curriculum. I would like to insert a personal opinion here that it might be a good idea for us to avoid the areas of *Lear* criticism which debate whether Shakespeare was a pagan of a Christian. (The last entry in the *Perplex*—174—does this, for instance, and Orwell—*P.* 90—makes a good case for Shakespeare as a non-religious humanist, but most critics opt for the Christian explanation.) I think our students know very little about the meaning of Christianity, and to analyze the play in terms of Christian-ness would require a large-scale introduction to religion.

Our students should be familiar with the political reasons for some of Shakespeare's adaptations from his sources, or the suggestions that some roles were enlarged because of the availability of certain actors, but the change he made in *Lear* was clearly a philosophical one, and Shakespeare's own idea, rather than that of his society. His is the only version in which Cordelia and Lear die, and after Shakespeare's death, Nahum Tate produced the most outrageous corruption of a Shakespeare text (its closing passages are the first entry in *P.*), a version which was played for two centuries, and approved of by so distinguished a critic as Samuel Johnson (*P.* 10). According to Tate's version, not only do Lear and Gloucester survive but Cordelia lives to marry Edgar, even though this last piece of chicanery makes it necessary to dispose of Cordelia's husband, one of the few really noble characters in the play.

This ending removed most of the horror of the play, in a manner we customarily assume is exclusive with the Hollywood of the twentieth century. It also satisfied, better than Shakespeare's text, the age-old requirement that a play involving a revolt against authority must end with a strong and legitimate royalty restored. Although Shakespeare stretches pretty far to get Fortinbras in at the end of *Hamlet,* he is clearly of royal blood, and Malcolm, youth that he may be, is of the blood royal, even though Macduff has to do the killing for him. But in *Lear*, Shakespeare deliberately defied those conventions he otherwise so scrupulously observed, with only a weak triumvirate of quasi-royal people—a suddenly reformed Albany, a king's in-law at best, and Kent and Edgar, mere noblemen. It is little wonder that the play's ending bothered the succeeding generations—not only was justice unrewarded but the sacred principle of royalty discarded. It must have been terribly important to Shakespeare to do this, and it seems to me the easiest way to explain it is to consider how much of the play's impact is removed by the Tate excision. Whether the metamorphosis of Lear may be described as Christian or Stoic or humanistic, clearly the author wants to show that it is so tremendous a change that, once he has been through his purgation, he *must* die. For him to continue to live would reduce the play immeasureably, and for him to be saved the ultimate horror of the death of his daughter would also diminish the extent of the horror that befalls him. Critical evaluation has discarded the "happy ending" of course, but the wonder is that it could have survived as long as it did.

Even though the two concurrent plots do not stand up under logical analysis, what happens to Lear and Gloucester does horrify us. What we are concerned with is not *how* it happens—to suggest that Lear's vanity or Gloucester's insults to his bastard son bring on their respective mistreatment also reduces the stature of the play—but *that* it happens. Each of these men is forced to the lowest possible estate in order to be brought to the highest one—the recognition of truth. Gloucester, according to a commonplace of critical analysis, begins to see in a spiritual sense at the moment that his eyes are brutally torn out, just as Lear reaches the ultimate of ecstasy only after being literally stripped of his royal trappings. The gimmickry of the plots that brings these epiphanies to pass is not as significant as the recognitions themselves.

Of course Lear's struggle is the primary one, even though his downfall occurs so early in the play, and Gloucester's problems are presented in more extended terms—the silly attempt at suicide over the Dover cliffs for instance—and it is not only that Lear is the title character. Although the play is about all human experience, it is in terms of a royal person, even though Samuel Johnson (*P.* 12) suggests that "it is disputed whether the predominant image in Lear's disordered mind be the loss of his kingdom or the cruelty of his daughters." Johnson's own conclusion: "Lear would move our compassion but little, did we not rather consider the injured father than the degraded king."

This lends to another possible paradox. If Lear's tragedy is in terms of ungrateful children, is it then a story of a private man rather than a public one? Here, too, since either answer can be given, we may say that neither is correct. Henry II's tradedy in *The Lion in Winter* is in terms of ungrateful or undutiful sons, as monarchs in Biblical tradition suffered. In the Greek tradition too, every giant-sized tragedy concerns an

essentially tiny problem—Agamemnon, Antigone, Medea, all
obsessed with sex or jealousy or loss of children.

We may resolve the paradox by saying that kings differ
from us ordinary folk only in the *size* of their anguish, since
they are king-size in everything. But the nature of their
anguish is that of all men. Although according to Elizabethan
tradition, goodness was defined in terms of loyalty to the
monarch (the Fool and Kent in *Lear* were loyal in spite of
great provocation to desert the cranky old man), the monarch is never safe from the ills that tend on ordinary men. It
is not only an Elizabethan convention, however, that fate of
kings and powerful men engages our attention, and that I
think is the underlying theme of the first unit, of which *Lear*
constitutes the capstone work.

Questions: *King Lear*

Write a paper on *one* of the following topics based on your
reading of *King Lear:*

I

This play begins at the moment when an established blindness in
two men is about to become an instrument of fate for the violent
opening of their eyes.[4]

John Masefield

As A.C. Bradley repeatedly notes, "the parallel between Lear
and Gloucester is, up to a certain point, so marked that it
cannot possibly be accidental."[5] These parallels (and contrasts) are obviously intended to deepen the king's portrayal
in his situation. Select as many parallels and contrasts as you
can develop that exist between Gloucester and Lear: in what
and who they are; in their situations; their tragedies; their
responses; their rhetoric. Support your assertions with specific allusions and textual citations.

or

II

Cordelia defies analysis as traditional heroine; yet she is more
than a dramatic device to illuminate her father's portrayal.

---

[4] Helmut Bonheim, ed., *The King Lear Perplex* (Belmont, California: Wadsworth
Publishing Co., 1960), p. 60.

[5] *Ibid.*, p. 48.

Depending upon his own character and tastes, the reader/viewer sees Cordelia in varying ways. Select the aspect of Cordelia which strikes you as most effective: as sister, as princess, as daughter, as queen, as martyr . . . or what you will. Develop a case for your view of Cordelia, supporting your argument with textual allusions and citations.

Answer both A *and* B.

A. At the end of the second act, with a storm gathering, Cornwall says to his host Gloucester

"Shut up your doors, my lord: 'tis a wild night."

Although this is on the surface just a reasonable request, it is of course far from a casual remark. Effectively delivered, it has a powerful, even shattering effect. Discuss what the implications of this line are, in respect to the structure of the play and the development of the play and theme. (How do you feel when Cornwall says this and why?)

B. Consider this speech of Lear's (Act III, Scene iv):

Poor naked wretches, wheresoe'er you are,
That bide the pelting of this pitiless storm.
How shall your houseless heads and unfed sides,
Your looped and windowed raggedness, defend you
From seasons such as these? O, I have taken
Too little care of this! Take physic,* pomp!
Expose thyself to feel what wretches feel,
That thou mayst shake the superflux** to them
And show the heavens more just.

*physic—medicine
**superflux—superfluity

Analyze this passage, beginning with a statement in your own words of the literal meaning and a brief explanation of its significance within the play, specifically what it shows about Lear's development. Continue with an analysis of the language of the passage—words or groups of words that are striking, and why you think they are. Consider such elements as word order, sound, unusual word coinage, or unusual word choice.

HUMANITIES: Suggestions for first written assignment

Discuss one of the following statements in a paper of

about 1000 words, including specific references to your reading or viewing during the summer, as well as references to the contemporary world.

1. A leader may be rejected by his people in spite of his success in terms of conquest or prosperity.
2. A leader may be acclaimed and beloved even while he defies or ignores the standard his people demand of themselves.
3. In defeat a leader may reach his greatest heights.
4. A people who destroy a leader may go on to idealize him afterwards.
5. In pursuit of a given cause, a leader may end by being remembered for encouraging a quite different one.
6. A man in public life may choose to honor a private motive over a public one, and in so doing achieve a desirable public good.
7. A group may reject a clearly well-qualified person because of some disquiet over a minor matter, and turn to a person who is less qualified and even positively disliked.
8. Prosperity may be accompanied by moral decay.
9. Out of adversity great constructive achievements may come.
10. A people may be willing to risk a great deal for what seems to be in terms of logic a trivial or useless cause.
11. A public figure may change drastically and unexpectedly in his ability to accept responsibility fully.
12. A good but weak man may be harmful to a society.
13. A bad but strong man may be helpful to a society.
14. The majority is always wrong.
15. The majority is always right.
16. The original thinker is doomed to be misunderstood.
17. The only worthwhile kind of new thinking is that which is understood by its audience.
18. A public figure's ideas may be taken by his followers in a way quite contrary to his original intentions or meaning.
19. Compromise is essential for political progress.
20. Compromise is a destructive force in society.

21. Intense family loyalty may create a dynasty that will be respected by a whole society.
22. A society seeks to imbue its leaders with a mystique which is essential to the society's needs.
23. A society sacrifices its leaders.
24. The function of a leader is to suffer for his people.
25. The function of a leader is to exist on a magnificent level beyond the reach of the ordinary member of his society.
26. A leader reflects his society; he who cannot do this, cannot become a leader.
27. A leader creates and moves his society; anyone who obtains power and does not do these things is not a leader.
28. The freer a society is, the greater its chances for stability.
29. The more authoritarian a social structure is, the greater its chances for stability.
30. The more stable a society, the more progress is likely to occur.
31. The more turmoil within a society, the more progress is likely to occur.
32. The more a person becomes involved with the mechanism of his society, the less likely he is to fulfill his own creative urges.
33. The more involved a person is with the workings of his society, the better he is able to live a creative life.
34. Real creativity can exist only with an attitude of aloofness from society.
35. The more self-interested a person, the less constructive a member of society.
36. The more self-interested a person, the more constructive a member of society.
37. Altruism is equivalent to self-destruction: an ideally altruistic society would destroy itself.
38. Altruism is the only possible basis for a strong society.
39. Traditions are essential to a constructive, dynamic society.
40. Traditions are harmful to the maintenance of a dynamic society.
41. A society needs institutions that transcend a man's life span.

THE PUBLIC MAN

Examine each of these comments upon the public man. Then discuss the one statement which strikes you as particularly valid in relation to your recent reading and observation:

> Some great men owe most of their greatness to the ability of detecting in those they destine for their tools the exact quality of strength that matters for their work.
>
> Joseph Conrad, *Lord Jim*

> A King is a thing men have made for their own sakes, for quietness' sake. Just as in a Family one man is appointed to buy the meat.
>
> John Selden (1584-1654),
> from "Of a King" in
> *Table Talk*

> When nature removes a great man, people explore the horizon for a successor; but none comes, and none will. His class is extinguished with him. In some other and quite different field, the next man will appear.
>
> Ralph Waldo Emerson,
> from *Uses of Great Men* (1850)

> The genius of a good leader is to leave behind him a situation which common sense, without the grace of genius, can deal with successfully.
>
> Walter Lippmann, from
> "Roosevelt Has Gone"
> April 14, 1945

> The people have always some champion whom they set over them and nurse into greatness . . . This and no other is the root from which a tyrant springs; when he first appears he is a protector.
>
> Plato, *The Republic*,
> Book VIII

The efficiency of the truly national leader consists primarily in preventing the division of the attention of a people, and always in concentrating it on a single enemy.

> Adolf Hitler, *Mein Kampf,*
> Volume I

To be a leader of men one must turn one's back on men.

> Havelock Ellis, from the
> introduction to Huysmans'
> *Against the Grain*

Man, who in his own selfish affairs is a coward to the backbone, will fight for an idea like a hero.

> George Bernard Shaw,
> *Man and Superman*, Act III

Great scoundrels have been beneficent rulers whilst amiable and privately harmless monarchs have ruled their countries by trusting to the hocus-pocus of innocence and guilt, reward and punishment, virtuous indignation and pardon, instead of standing up to the facts without either malice or mercy.

> George Bernard Shaw,
> preface to *Major Barbara*

> What infinite heart's ease
> Must kings neglect that private men enjoy!
> And what have kings that privates have not too,
> Save ceremony, save general ceremony?
> And what art thou, thou idol Ceremony?
> What kind of god art thou, that suffer'st more
> Of mortal griefs than do thy worshipers?

> Shakespeare,
> King Henry in *Henry V*

Reference Points for Machiavelli, *The Prince*

Since introductions to *The Prince* accompany most editions, I shall restrict these remarks to some indication of the scope of the subject and suggestions as to ways in which this work may be used by the teacher.

Niccolo Machiavelli (1469-1527) was contemporaneous with many of the major events of the Italian Renaissance and some of its most memorable people. The famous Medici family flourished in Machiavelli's home city of Florence. Lorenzo the Magnificent held absolute power in Florence until 1492 although the city was outwardly a republic. The famous Medici Pope Leo X bore the brunt of the initial revolt of Martin Luther. There were the infamous Borgias: the father, Pope Alexander VI; the son, Cesare Borgia; the daughter, Lucretia. This was the era of Michelangelo, Raphael, Botticelli and countless others. There was the fanatic religious reformer Savonarola, who influenced the Florentines to give up their luxuries for a short time.

When Savonarola was executed in 1498, Machiavelli was elected Secretary to the Chancery of the Republic of Florence, the institution which controlled both foreign and military affairs. The young secretary had the opportunity to observe practical politics; he took part in 24 missions abroad visiting France, Rome, and the Holy Roman Empire among others. These thirteen years had been a low point for the Medici family: when the French threatened Florence again, the Medici family was recalled and Machiavelli was punished and exiled.

An interesting contrast can be drawn between Machiavelli, exiled to a small piece of property outside Florence, watching the countryside at work, joining in dice and cards with villagers, spending the evenings with the Greats in print, and Italy experiencing catastrophe after catastrophe. He saw Charles V of the Holy Roman Empire and Spain (known there as Charles I) and Francis I of France struggle for the control of Italy, one pawn in the game of power. His conclusions as to what Italians could do about the situation are the kernel of *The Prince,* written in 1513. In it he dreamed that someday Italy would be a New Monarchy similar to Spain, France or England of his day, when her people would fight together for patriotic causes and uphold her dignity before Europe, when Italy would find a Leader, and *The Prince* would be a handbook for him. Under what conditions should he seize power? How should he use that power once it had been acquired? What difficulties would arise before, during and after power had been seized by the Leader, the Prince?

There are other reasons for the fame of *The Prince.* It did not describe things as they should be, but as they were. It was secular, scientific, modern. "The state was not the guardian of any universal, God-given or natural law, but a human device inseparable from human needs and passions, based on force, not right."

These ideas usher in the modern world, and bury the medieval. Their repercussions echoed through Europe, in the essays of Montaigne, in the *First Anniversary* of Donne, and above all, in the tragedies of Shakespeare, where the splitting of appearance and reality, and the confrontation with man's true nature and destiny take on their widest and deepest dimensions. Among the truths to which they lead—and this is the one in which Machiavelli was most interested—is the necessity for man, with his dual nature, to live simultaneously in two worlds, the political and the moral. Each has its claims on us. Yet their natures are apparently so different that we have not yet succeeded, and perhaps never can succeed, in fusing them.

Quotations from *The Prince:*

1. " . . . a prudent man should always follow in the path trodden by great men and imitate those who are most excellent, so that if he does not attain to their greatness, at any rate he will get some tinge of it."

Is this the path to greatness? Do great men follow a "path" that anyone can follow? Who are the "great men" others should follow? How can we determine who they are?

2. "A prince need trouble little about conspiracies when the people are well disposed, but when they are hostile and hold him in hatred, then he must fear everything and everybody."
   " . . . the best fortress is to be found in the love of the people, for although you may have fortresses, they will not save you if you are hated by the people."

Does Machiavelli ever explain how "the people" learn to love a leader? Are "the people" the same today as in Machiavelli's time?

3. " . . . if one waits till (discords) are at hand, the medicine is no longer in time as the malady has become incurable."
   " . . . one ought never to allow a disorder to take place in order to avoid war, for war is not thereby avoided, but only deferred to your disadvantage."

What is your reaction to this argument? How might Machiavelli react to police methods in our cities today? What suggestions do you have to prevent matters reaching a climax such as Machiavelli describes?

4. "A man who wishes to make a profession of goodness in everything must necessarily come to grief among so many who are not good. Therefore, it is necessary . . .to learn how not to be good, and to use this knowledge and not use it, according to the necessity of the case."

Describe the man who might be capable of acting in this manner. Can you think of any other possible reaction, given a society in which so many are not good? What happens when a whole society believes in this principle?

5. " . . . liberality such as the world understands it will injure you, because if used virtuously and in the proper way, it will not be known, and you will incur the disgrace of the contrary vice."

What is Machiavelli suggesting here? Admitting there is some truth in this quote, is there any other alternative a liberal person has?

HISTORIOGRAPHY:

Machiavelli–Cynic, Patriot or Political Scientist?[6] (Heath Series) is a slim volume of fairly extensive quotations from famous critical works on Machiavelli. Some examples follow from pages xv and xvi:

1. Frederick II (The Great)
   "I venture now to take up the defence of humanity against this monster who wants to destroy it; with reason and justice I dare to oppose sophistry and crime; and I put forth these reflections on *The Prince* of Machiavelli, chapter by chapter, so that the antidote may be found immediately following the poison."

2. Max Lerner
   "May I venture a guess as to the reason why we still shudder slightly at Machiavelli's name? It is not only the tradition I have described. It is our recognition that the realities he described ARE realities; that men, whether in politics, in business or in private life, do NOT act according to their professions of virtue."

---

[6]De Lamar Jensen, ed., *Machiavelli–Cynic, Patriot or Political Scientist?* (Lexington, Mass.: D.C. Heath and Co., 1960).

3. Pasquale Villari

"When, on completing this analysis ... Machiavelli proceeds to draw his conclusions, then at last the practical side and real aim of his work are clearly seen. It is a question of achieving the unity of his Italian motherland and of delivering it from foreign rule ... "

4. L.A. Burd

"The Prince was never meant except for Italians, and Italians too of a given period; indeed, we may go further, and ask whether it was ever intended even for all Italians; it certainly bears the stamp of what a modern writer might call an esoteric treatise."

5. Ernst Cassirer

"The Prince is neither a moral nor an immoral book; it is simply a technical book. In a technical book we do not seek rules of ethical conduct, of good or evil."

6. Joseph Kraft

"Not so clean and neat ... is the contention that Machiavelli, a dispassionate observer of the facts, is the Darwin of politics. Rather this contention is messy with black marks. Machiavelli did not observe the facts closely. His deductions were, in many cases, illogical. He utterly misread the general military picture of the day ... The poor man appears to be as much a poet as a scientist."

7. G.P. Gooch

"Despite the number and eminence of his disciples, I believe that Machiavelli is unfair to mankind. The professed realist only saw a limited portion of the vast field of experience. The will to power is not the sole key to human nature ... "

GENERAL QUESTIONS:

1. Why did Machiavelli write *The Prince?*
This question should develop into a discussion of motivation—in this case, the possible motivations of a man in exile, filled with hate, envy, love? But the possible answers may lead into motivation in general—of politicians—of ourselves?

2. Does *The Prince* read as if one person wrote the entire book?

Perhaps they will notice a difference between the last chapter and the remainder of the book. They might go on to account for the difference in tone, style, etc.

3. How could Machiavelli see Cesare Borgia as "the hero"?
This discussion would be based on chapter 7 in which Machiavelli eulogizes Cesare. This will help to clarify question 1 above, as well as lead to an understanding of different people's needs for heroes with particular characteristics. What kind of person might need this kind of hero?

4. Which type of government does Machiavelli favor? What are his reasons?
The whole pragmatic nature of the book should come through very clearly here—Machiavelli's ability to look at things as they are, not as he might have liked them to be.

5. Do Machiavelli's ideas on leadership satisfy you?
Are the characteristics of leaders he stresses the "right" ones? Is there a mold for leadership?

6. Machiavelli writes of how a Prince should appear to be, rather than what he is. Do we share this hypocrisy? Would you want it any differently? Can it be different? Is there any public figure who disproves the thesis?

7. How does Machiavelli fit into the mainstream of his time? Why?

THE HUMANITIES AND SCHOOL MORALE

By no means should the statement and exploration of goals become the exclusive concern of the humanities team. At every stage along the route to the development and implementation of a humanities curriculum, as many of the entire faculty as possible should be invited to make suggestions, to criticize, and to participate. Some of the leaders in the faculty association should be more than invited—they should be sought out and urged to contribute their talents. A humanities curriculum can adversely affect the rest of the school if only the teaching team receives attention and praise. Morale can be shattered if one group of teachers, and one class of students, are enjoying extra benefits while the majority of the school is neglected. Several patterns of behavior are recommended:

1. All announcements of humanities planning sessions should be posted on the faculty bulletin board.

2. Special invitations should be extended to teachers when discussions dealing with their areas of competence are to be reviewed. (For example, foreign language teachers should be involved when a book like Cervantes' *Don Quixote* is considered; science teachers when dealing with Darwin's *Origin of Species,* etc.)

3. Never plan to remove students in the humanities program from other classes for all-day trips, etc., without first consulting affected teachers. Make certain that the purpose of the trip is a valid one and cannot be accomplished by other means.

4. A schedule of each week's humanities program should be provided each teacher in the school. In this way the regular faculty can share in the bounty of outside speakers, films, and other special features available through the humanities program. And when the teacher brings his freshmen, sophomores, and juniors to the humanities class, these students are made more fully aware of this elective choice than they would be by merely reading about the humanities elective in a bulletin.

5. Where possible, members of the faculty outside the humanities staff should be asked to give guest lectures and serve as resource people.

6. Students in the humanities curriculum who have completed special projects should be made available as resource people for teachers in courses where such projects could be explained or demonstrated (dramatic and dance groups, work on Greek history, renaissance paintings, visits to museums, etc.).

As much as humanly possible, the entire school—students, faculty, and parents—must be kept aware of the humanities curriculum's benefits for everyone. Senior students not in the humanities curriculum still need to be invited to free or low-cost drama programs, concerts, and special student-led shows. We made a silly error during the first year in neglecting to offer so simple a courtesy to students who had not elected the humanities curriculum.

Once the innovators of a humanities curriculum are removed or alienated from the mainstream of faculty and students, the program is doomed. In schools where the position of departmental chairman is a strong one the need to make certain that these people are not opposed to the humanities curriculum is absolutely essential. With some justification, many of these chairmen see in the humanities curriculum a challenge to their unitary authority. When an English chairman schedules a departmental meeting and an English teacher must decline because he has a previously arranged session with the humanities team, trouble can be anticipated. Administrators should exert all their efforts to offer chairmen the wider perspective that makes the humanities curriculum a viable school-wide program. And teachers in the humanities curriculum must be sensitized to recognize that their special responsibilities are not divorced from the jurisdiction of their departmental chairman.

One way to avoid serious confrontations between subject loyalties and the obligations inherent in membership in a humanities team is in making judicious teacher assignments. Where possible, teachers in the humanities curriculum should be involved with regular subjects as well. And arrangements can be made not to have meetings of the humanities staff conflict with subject department schedules. One of the better solutions is to have one or more of the department chairmen serve as participating members of a humanities staff. Another is to rotate the regular staff so that the humanities team never becomes, or is felt by the rest of the faculty to be, an exclusive monopoly. Changing teachers each year offers many commendable features. New teachers mean new ideas. The humanities curriculum will not suffer from a hardening of the syllabus. New teachers mean new opportunities to acquaint additional staff members with fresh approaches to learning outside of the traditional classroom setting. Veterans of the humanities team who return to their classrooms will never teach their regular classes in the exact traditional format again. Although changing the humanities teaching team is desirable, the personalities as well as competencies of the teachers must be the foremost concern when selecting the humanities faculty. Wisdom decrees that a humanities veteran is preferred for a second or third year to a new teacher who cannot adjust to the open humanities environment,—and some teachers are so natural for a humanities curriculum that they should almost never be removed!

One final warning on the humanities curriculum and morale: an administrator should not become so galvanized and committed to the humanities curriculum that other important areas of the school receive lesser attention. The tendency for the administrator, if he wishes to help the humanities program succeed, will be to attend the planning sessions, participate in discussions, and in general, make his presence felt. Alas, administrators, by the very nature of their positions, can quickly "take over" a project. To indicate too much interest is to be accused of meddling or distrusting the staff. On the other hand, to leave the humanities program completely alone is to face the charge of apathy and neglect. Achieving a balanced view and level of support is the impossible golden mean. Indeed so many factors must be considered when a school moves from the traditional subject-centered curriculum to a humanistic model that the desire to see the proposal through can fade very quickly. Everyone and everything has to be considered: the students, the teachers, the administrative staff, the board of education, the parents, the scheduling problems, the room assignments, the clerical tasks, and lots more. But not to try is to face a charge like the following from students:

> At our school there is an over-emphasis on grades coupled with a keen sense of competition among the student body, and this is having a profound effect on us all. We do not feel that we have an ideal atmosphere in which to mature and pass the growing stages of life. School only adds to our general anxiety and uncertainty.
>
> Now is the time when we want to probe, to discover, and in general, to look around. Instead, school emphasizes the academics. Unfortunately, as we go from subject to subject the discussion has only been minutely on individual exploration, which is true learning. Mostly we have "book-learning" which is memory by rote ... We need to see a greater concern for individual growth and independent, original work. Students should not be taught to; they should be instilled with the desire to learn, and they should be taught how to learn—but the process of learning is strictly an individual affair, dependent on individual motivation. ... It is more important to know a reference source for a formula and its possible applications, than to just be able to memorize that formula ...

More than 50 years ago Alfred North Whitehead, writing on this same theme, phrased the problem more eloquently:

There is only one subject-matter for education, and that is Life in all its manifestations. Instead of this single unity, we offer children—Algebra, from which nothing follows; Geometry, from which nothing follows; Science, from which nothing follows; History, from which nothing follows; a Couple of Languages, never mastered; and lastly, most dreary of all, Literature, represented by plays of Shakespeare, with philological notes and short analyses of plot and character to be in substance committed to memory. Can such a list be said to represent Life, as it is known in the midst of the living of it? The best that can be said of it is, that it is a rapid table of contents which a deity might run over in his mind while he was thinking of creating a world, and has not yet determined how to put it together.[7]

A humanities curriculum can educate for life. But too many well-intentioned programs have floundered by combining humanistic studies with inhuman action toward those both in and out of the program. Inevitably the hypocrisy between theory and practice is exposed. A humanistic curriculum must be lived, not just expounded. Here, for example, is a verbatim tape of how the humanities team shared experiences and ideas in their conference periods:

English teacher: "In our seminar yesterday, the students compared Hector and Achilles. Some characterized Hector as a 'group man,' a demi-god who was loyal to his family and his country. Others saw Achilles as a loner. You played the game his way or you didn't play at all."

Social studies teacher: "None of us thought of making this kind of comparison in our seminar session. I'll raise the question with them on Friday."

Drama teacher: "One of our students claimed that if Achilles was living today he would be called 'chicken' by his countrymen for refusing to fight. But a chorus of youngsters insisted that there was nothing dishonorable in refusing to fight if you did not respect the leader.—And this in turn led to an all-out discussion on what was honorable and dishonorable to the Greeks then and to us today."

If the humanities help man become more human, and they do, the total pattern of organization, concern, and implementation

---

[7] Alfred North Whitehead, *The Aims of Education* (New York: The Free Press, 1967), p. 7.

must be humanistically conceived and humanistically administered. To borrow from the Vista advertisements, "If a school is
not part of the solution, it is part of the problem."

Knowledge alone is not enough. The primary characteristic of a
fine teacher must be a spirit of respect, indeed reverence for
students. While it is spurious to claim the superiority of intention
and instinct over intellect, our schools have thrown far greater
emphasis on knowledge than knowledge alone merits. Erich
Fromm, in *The Art of Loving*, a book all teachers should make a
part of their working vocabulary and lives, states the point best:

> While we teach knowledge, we are losing that teaching which is
> the most important one for human development: the teaching
> which can only be given by the simple presence of a mature,
> loving person. In previous epochs of our own culture, or in China
> and India, the man most highly valued was the person with
> outstanding spiritual qualities. Even the teacher was not only, or
> even primarily, a source of information, but his function was to
> convey certain human attitudes . . .[8]

[8]Erich Fromm, *The Art of Loving* (New York: Harper and Row, Inc., Bantam edition, 1963), p. 98.

CHAPTER 6

Organizing a Humanities Curriculum
–Phase Two

What happens when teachers representing different disciplines come together to develop an integrated, uncommon curriculum? Even when the teachers are the best of friends, trouble can be anticipated. Integration, in curriculum content as in life, is easier to legislate than to realize. Each discipline has a special rationale of its own. Teachers who are steeped in the structure of their respective subjects will not lightly yield their special interests. Only when the thinking transcends the myopia of separate disciplines and the focus of interest moves to a larger common denominator can a humanities curriculum become truly viable.

Problems are further exacerbated by the unfortunate major and minor labels colleges and schools attach to each discipline. For reasons that echo society's priority of values, mathematics, science, foreign language, history and English are considered major subjects. Music, drama, art, dance, photography, sculpture and design are called and treated as minors. Too many major subject teachers have been conditioned to feel superior and to act in a patronizing manner to their minor subject colleagues. And the latter are often overly defensive in asserting their proper claim to a student's time.

An administrator will have to utilize all his charm, patience, sympathy, pressure, and prayers to bring a divergent staff together. But this is precisely what being a school administrator is all about. To refuse to enter the lion's den of teacher dissent and distrust is to be accused of making no difference in the life of the school. Some of the preliminary faculty sessions will produce much rhetoric and much doubt about the wisdom of continuing the discussions. The academic heat will be intense; the light will be diffused. Such meetings will remind the school administrator of an old definition: A meeting is a gathering of important people who singly can do nothing, but together can decide that nothing can be done. Every initiative that promises cooperation and movement in fresh directions will have to be seized by the administrator and pushed for all it's worth.

Four examples of diverse views on establishing a school's humanities program are cited below. They illustrate the depth of thinking and the types of conflicts that can be contemplated when teachers in English, social studies, music and art combine their talents to create a multidisciplinary curriculum. Although each teacher offers a humanistic rather than a narrow framework, disagreements on style and scope and even philosophy are evident. We will then see how such conflicts can be resolved.

TEACHER COMMENTS ON THE HUMANITIES

From an English teacher:

O.K., we want to provide our seniors (and their teachers) with a school experience that will be more meaningful than that provided by the fragmented school day. We want to create a year which will be simultaneously capstone and foundation stone. It should build upon what they have already learned but cannot provide a conclusive answer to any fundamental questions. They must leave this program full of unanswered questions, enough to last their whole lifetimes.

We are lucky to have students who want to learn, although this desire takes different forms. Some yearn for information; others for meanings. A humanities curriculum must establish that these two goals are interrelated and interdependent. *Meaning,* which we all seek, teachers no less than students, is just as much involved with such matters as fact, history, tone, style, form, and technique as it is with theme and relevance to contemporary life. But it would be unfortunate if we were to say at the outset that this program will teach the meaning of life. At best, let us hope it will lead our seniors to the same attitude that their best teachers have, that learning is a life-long occupation. It is, in fact, what we think life is.

Now, nearly all teachers claim that these goals have always been theirs. And it is quite true that the conventional school day has produced and is continuing to produce these admirable educational outcomes. As I have said many times, isn't our principal the product of such a schooling? And aren't most of the rest of us who are struggling to create this new approach?

How can the interdisciplinary approach produce a whole greater than the sum of its component parts? How can the larger block of time be justified? It will, after all, take up a great deal of time that our current seniors idle away, in free periods, in walking from room to room, in dreaming through classes. These longer sessions cannot become simply periods for dreaming (though goodness knows the lazy daydreams of the young may be more valuable than any imposed activities from the adult world) that last a few hours rather than 40 minutes. Each long session must be planned carefully and yet be open enough to allow for unexpected responses that may not have occurred to the planners. Whatever the group does as a whole must spark individual activities which take advantage of the individual's special interests and abilities while at the same time pointing up the interdisciplinary nature of life and art.

I have been thinking of an approach which would use a specific-to-general sequence rather than a general-to-specific. Rather than to start out with some grand theme and persuade the students to see this theme dealt with by several disciplines, I would suggest beginning with a work of art that the whole group would see. Each of these artistic experiences would represent in itself the interrelationships of disciplines and lead to investigations of this and other works in respect to technique, style, history, theme.

Some works I have in mind at the moment are the following:

I. *Becket,* the film made from Jean Anouilh's play.

II. *Oedipus the King,* the film made by the Stratford, Canada Shakespeare Company; and the oratorio *Oedipus Rex* by Stravinsky, either in recording (preferably with the Cocteau narration) or in performance by the New York City Center Opera Company, where it has been in the regular repertory.

III. *Hamlet,* in the film by Laurence Olivier—or perhaps in addition to a current production.

IV. Picasso's painting *Guernica* and the artist's preliminary sketches, as on view at the Museum of Modern Art and in several texts.

CASE STUDY

Becket: possibilities for development

Besides being attractive enough in terms of recency, cast, and critical success, this film may be considered in all these categories:

1. A twentieth century history play by a Frenchman
2. A discussion of the problem of church-state relations
3. A re-creation of a twelfth century event
4. An investigation of some of the paradoxes of historical progress
5. A psychological study

Now these five categories, all of which may in some degree overlap, may be further subdivided and expanded:

a. *A 20th century history play by a Frenchman.* As a play by Anouilh, it could lead to further study of this playwright's works, his language, his serious and farcical works. It could also lead into a study of other French dramatists.

b. As a play about Becket, it immediately suggests T.S. Eliot's *Murder in the Cathedral.* Contrasting these two should illuminate the special qualities and idea of commitment of the two playwrights, and of their respective places in the twentieth century. This could also include a student production of the Eliot play or a trip to see a production, or listening to the recording. It could lead to a further study of Eliot's poetry.

c. As a history play, it could lead to a study of other twentieth century history plays; why did other writers choose other historical characters?—Bolt's *A Man for All Seasons,* for instance, or Osborne's *Luther.*

d. As a history play, it could lead to a study of past examples of the genre—ideal to see the Olivier films or the educational television series of Shakespeare—*(Henry V, Rich-are III).*

... The more I write, the more tangled the problems of procedure begin to loom in my mind. I do see some possibilities in the "Sample Works" approach, as long as it is not called "Great Works" or "Great Books." These are of course great works, but I could see almost any set of works being used, always depending on the degree of interest in them that the teachers involved have. We are aiming always at an *introduction* to these works, with the assumption that any of these may be seen or heard or viewed over and over again by students and teachers in the future, and that what we are doing in this course is to suggest that such re-viewing is important to a good life. Thus, it is important that the teachers involved find enough interest in these works themselves, enough interest to discuss them or entertain new thoughts about them, or else we will not have proved our thesis to the students. In this connection, I would leave time and space in the schedule for all sorts of unpredicted or unexpected tie-ins, events or concepts that come up, in the world at large or in newspapers or magazines, and which further the thought that humanities is a way of looking at life and not just at a specific work.

I would also suggest that, whatever plan is adopted, room in the schedule be left for taking advantage of cultural or historical events that may occur in the course of the year and that may fit effectively into the senior curriculum.

[Note how many discipline fields are encompassed and how exciting are the suggestions from the English teacher. Many of her subject colleagues would be more insistent on simple book coverage with story-line and character emphasis. Note, too, how the appeal is primarily to the intellect, a faith in the powers of the mind.]

From a social studies teacher:

The following is not in any way intended as a rebuttal to the excellent suggestions offered which I consider really brilliant in almost all respects. Rather, it is most sketchily detailed below as another approach, i.e., from an examination of a general hypothesis to the specifics (only a few, to be sure) in an effort to *raise* but not to *solve* some meaningful questions.

One thing bothers me about the *Becket* format. From a central artistic experience, i.e., the viewing of the film, various groups charge off in different directions which become increasingly fragmented as they go deeper into their study. It seems to be a fan which spreads out farther and farther away from its vertex. I wonder if simply seeing *Becket* again at the end is enough to successfully pull all the disparate blades of the fan together? I wonder if such a structure doesn't perhaps lay too heavy a burden on *any* masterwork *per se?* (One might even question whether or not *Becket*, the film, qualifies, but that's not really the point.) Although I tried hard, I couldn't find any overarching theme, generalization or hypothesis, or the plural of any of these. Nor did I really find unification of disciplines within each specialized study group. The only conjunction of all these planets occurs at the end, when everyone steps back several steps to *Becket* itself. We may well decide that this is enough; I'm just raising the questions.

The general-to-specifics approach has king-sized pitfalls of its own. While the format virtually guarantees the performance of solid work within each group, the ideational theme, if we're not awfully careful, can result only in the performance of solid flab. The choice of illustrative examples can be forced, specious, capricious or otherwise just plain lousy. Assuming that we *could* avoid THE PIT(S), one advantage might be that each group, in marching off from the center, will be nibbling at different petals of the *same plant,* so that reporting and exchange will be clearly relevant. Another advantage could be that each study group will experience a *range* of activities, although there could easily be some specialization within each group.

Here's a sample theme-to-test, hypothesis or whatever: (Note that I have not really tried to suggest appropriate art, music or dance experiences for each group because I'm not competent to do so. I also assume that relevant history will incidentally, and *only* incidentally, accompany each work to validate it in time, place and meaning.)

Reinhold Niebuhr,"MAN, ALONE, IS MORAL. COLLECTIVE MAN IS FOREVER IMMORAL."[1]

Group I:
    To test this proposition: MAN, ALONE, IS MORAL.
    Possible Activities:
    A. See film *A Man for All Seasons*. The moral man in action.
    B. Discuss Prometheus myth.
    C. Read, perhaps do scenes from *The Last Angry Man*.
    D. Excerpts from Locke, Rousseau. Man in a state of nature is beautiful.
    E. Read, discuss, existentialists Kierkegaard, Sartre. Man can find his meaning only for and by himself.

Group II:
    To test this proposition: MAN, ALONE, IS IMMORAL.
    Possible activities:
    A. See the film *Hud*. Man can be entirely immoral; nice guys contribute.
    B. Read Hobbes *The Leviathan,* or excerpts from it. Man in a state of nature is entirely selfish and brutal.
    C. Read, see, perform, *The Bad Seed* or *Turn of the Screw*.
    D. Read Freud on the id, socializing effects of society, development of the superego.

Group III:
    To test this proposition: COLLECTIVE MAN IS FOREVER IMMORAL.
    Possible activities:
    A. "Genesis," on the expulsion from Eden.
    B. Selections from Luther and Calvin, on original sin.
    C. de Tocqueville, on the cynicism and meaninglessness of relationships among the mass.
    D. Ardrey's *African Genesis,* positing the predatory-ape origins of man.
    E. French film *We Are All Murderers,* damning the immorality of society in terms of capital punishment, an eye for an eye.

---

[1]Reinhold Niebuhr, *Moral Man and Immoral Society* (New York: Charles Scribner's Sons, 1932).

Group IV:

> To test this proposition: COLLECTIVE MAN IS (OR
> COULD BE) FOREVER MORAL.

Possible activities:

> A. Jefferson on the improvability of man, Condorcet on
> the perfectibility of man, through society.
> B. Proudhon or some other Utopian socialist.
> C. *Major Barbara,* on perfectibility of society through
> technology.
> D. Diego Rivera's murals.

It would be great if during the reporting, there would be hassles and rebuttals. *African Genesis* may make some students so angry that they will be driven to read a traditional anthropologist's account of man's origins. Another group may get annoyed enough at Luther's smug arrogation of right to himself that they will take a look at the biography and play that sees him as a constipated neurotic. I would hope for majority and minority reports from each group, who may not have been sold by their exploration, and may agree and disagree a hundred times with one another and with other groups. To sensitize them to ideas requiring some tentative judgment, through many different experiences, is the purpose of the whole humanities curriculum.

I'm far from satisfied with any of the above, and I am positive the group can find dozens of better illustrations.

[Again we have an example of a scholarly, wide ranging interpretation of the humanities whose focus is one of questioning, understanding, and meaning. Traditionally oriented social studies teachers would champion a chronological rather than a thematic design.]

From a fine arts teacher: (After a long session of the teaching team in which no real consensus was reached)

The point that disturbed me about our last meeting on the humanities was our seeming inability to be "honest with ourselves," as suggested by one of our more fearless faculty members. I will try to be honest.

The plan we draw up must be *more specific* than many of us seem to want, rather than what is more likely in projects such as this, to be less specific in order to satisfy everyone. Some teachers can teach the most meaningful of lessons with the most vague of concepts, the most nebulous of ideas, on paper, and these are usually the more experienced and most confident of teachers. But there are too many teachers who, when asked to teach with a vague idea of the content of the course, end up with aimless discussion on the theme because of either their lack of training or their inability to take vague concepts and translate them into practical classroom use. Given these variations in faculty, the more specific we get on paper, the better.

[The legitimate cry for specificity will be matched by the equally legitimate cry for more breadth and freedom. The background and attitude of each teacher will determine the angle and depth of the cry. To illustrate how each teacher's unique contributions change a humanities program, the following statement prepared by a *music teacher* describes a different mood and emphasis.]

Music in the humanities curriculum should be approached as an art reacting to and used by its environment. Instead of adhering to a strict chronological (primitive to modern) structure, twentieth century music should be discussed as it relates to and develops from previous periods. Music workshops would be concerned with the artist's role in society: how he uses his environment, the prevailing political and social attitutes, the degree of economic support and sponsorship of the arts, the effects of ruralization and urbanization, and how the integration of the arts attempts to create new musical forms.

Any course in precursors of contemporary music would include a study of French society at the turn of the century (marvelous flying machines, magnificently adorned women, amazing motor cars and homemade aquatic vehicles capable of dazzling speeds). Experimentation with impressionism, the beginnings of modern dance, and the invention of film would all contribute ideas to and elicit responses from musical composers.

Students of music would work in several areas, using anything from clutter to advertising's grotesqueries for musical improvisations and researched events. Participation in dance, theater, art, poetry, film and happenings could be included in a musical theme. The avant-garde music of each period should be related to the works of such artists as Stravinsky, Cage, La Monte Young, and Warhol. Classes should design their own sound environments and evolve contemporary uses of music through research, critical opinion, and experimentation.

From a second fine arts teacher:

A Multi-Media Experiment as Part of the Humanities Program

It is not in content but approach that we must concentrate our efforts. The world outside is exciting and frustrating and more often than not there are no immediate solutions, no right or wrong answers. The visual impact of TV, motion pictures, and other mass media are what's happening. Less orientation is needed to comprehend the visual image than is needed for the verbal or the written word. The "Generation Gap" is technological. The movie is a more intimate media, its communication more immediate, its content more relative to our own experiences. Youth wants and needs involvement, and not on a peripheral basis. The day of the teacher-directed experience is as out-of-date as the horse and buggy. Let me say, I believe the teacher must guide, direct and provoke thinking, but by using techniques other than those being presently employed in the fragmented school day. The students' most immediate needs are related to their own problems: self-identity is essential before addressing ourselves to the problems of others. As a part of the humanities program I would like to have the students make a movie. This would involve script writing, editing, acting, dancing and language in an engaging media that is representative of this generation. Films could be shown and discussed for meaning and content as well as technical and aesthetic considerations.

[We see here the desire to use the young technology of today as avenues for creative explorations. The conflict between the verbal and the visceral, between those who interpret the humanities as a cognitive experience and those who wish to develop the affective and aesthetic domains is a constant concern.]

SCHEDULING A HUMANITIES CURRICULUM

Flexibility in scheduling is one of the hallmarks of an effective humanities curriculum. Teachers and students must not be slaves to a bell that rings every 50 minutes and forces classes to end no matter how animated, no matter how crucial the discussion. With 60 students or more available for scheduling in the morning hours and another 60 or more students available in the afternoon, an administrator can assign an English and social studies teaching team to these two groups of students for a double or triple period each day. In this way the nature of the lesson will determine when a lesson should end. Nor does this type of flexible scheduling necessitate a radical restructuring in teacher programming. Assume for a moment that no humanities curriculum existed. To have scheduled the 60 students for regular classes in English would have required that an English teacher be assigned a minimum of two large classes of 30 each or a more reasonable class load of 20 to 25 each period if we wished to have the student-teacher ratio conform to the recommendations of the National Council of Teachers of English.[2] A comparable student-teacher ratio would prevail for the same 60 students scheduled for social studies. Here, for example is a typically separated English-social studies teacher-and-student schedule:

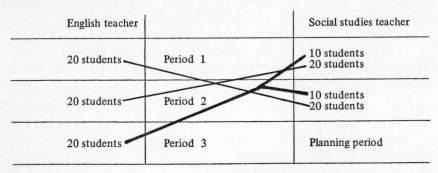

English teacher		Social studies teacher
20 students	Period 1	10 students / 20 students
20 students	Period 2	10 students / 20 students
20 students	Period 3	Planning period

Here now are the same 60 students and the English and social studies teachers in a humanities team:

---

[2]Resolution passed by the National Council of Teachers of English, Champaign, Ill., at the fifty-sixth Annual Meeting, 1966: "Class Load of the English Teacher—The Council has reaffirmed its position that the daily teaching load of the secondary school teacher of English be limited to four classes and a maximum of 100 students."

English and Social Studies Teachers

Period 1)
Period 2)—60 students
Period 3)

Organizing a team-taught humanities curriculum then is a matter of administrative scheduling so that student and teacher programs are meshed.

In the first year of a humanities curriculum, the need for the teaching team to make plans to evaluate and to change directions is almost a daily necessity. The teachers therefore must have time built into their schedule for a conference period each day. And if the program is to be given a chance to truly prosper, the English and social studies teachers should not be assigned to more than one daily class preparation in addition to a full morning or afternoon humanities schedule. In a typical five-class-period teaching day the humanities teaching team program might resemble the following:

English and Social Studies A.M. Humanities Team

Period 1)
Period 2)—Humanities
Period 3)
Period 4—Lunch
Period 5—Joint Conference Period
Period 6—English Class—Grades 8, 9 or 10
           Social studies teacher Free
Period 7—Social studies Class—Grades 8, 9 or 10
           English teacher Free
Official Class Duties

Teachers in the P.M. Humanities Team would follow a reversed schedule. Schools on an eight period day with budgets not overly restricted could make provision to have both the A.M. and the P.M. humanities team meet at the same time during the school day for a daily conference period. The advantages of such cross-fertilization of ideas for both humanities teams are obvious.

At Hunter, a single conference period each day proved inadequate. Additional time had to be arranged after the regular school day ended. At least once each week sessions of the entire humanities staff would continue until the dinner hour and beyond. In the second year of the humanities curriculum, budgetary restrictions made it impossible to provide the staff with even a planning period time allowance each day. Both the English and social studies teachers taught two lower grade classes in their discipline as well as assuming responsibility for the three period humanities curriculum. As a result the teaching teams worked far longer in preparing for the humanities program after school hours than any school administrator or community has a right to ask. That the staff did so willingly, even eagerly, testifies to their commitment.

But a humanities curriculum requires more than an English and social studies team. Ways have to be provided for the teachers in such disciplines as music, drama, dance and art to become active participants in the program. Maneuvering schedules to take account of this need can make what is educationally desirable, administratively possible. In a school with 60 or more students in the humanities curriculum a qualified teacher in each of the four disciplines could be assigned to a five period humanities program each week, as well as assigned to teach 15 to 20 other regular class periods. Again, in the first year of a humanities curriculum the art, music, drama and dance teachers must have time allotted during the school day to confer with each other and the English and social studies teaching team. Actually the so-called free time for conference sessions will rapidly melt away as students and teachers find that they require more and more time during and after school to discuss projects and revise programs.

In the first year of the humanities curriculum an art teacher's schedule might take this pattern:

Periods	Monday	Tuesday	Wednesday	Thursday	Friday
1	Humanities	8th grade Art I	Humanities	8th grade Art I	Humanities
2	Free	Free	7th grade Art I	8th grade Art I	Humanities
3	7th grade Art I	7th grade Art I	7th grade Art I	Free	Humanities
4	LUNCH			LUNCH	

Periods	Monday	Tuesday	Wednesday	Thursday	Friday
5			HUMANITIES CONFERENCE		
6	10th grade Art I	Free	10th grade Art I	10th grade Art I	8th grade Art II
7	10th grade Art I	Free	10th grade Art I	8th grade Art II	8th grade Art II

NOTE: 7th grade art meets four times a week, 8th grade art meets three times a week, 10th grade art meets five times a week.

Teachers in drama and music would follow the same single period. humanities schedule on Monday and Wednesday and the three humanities periods on Friday. Such a schedule provides students and teachers with a variety of options in choosing projects and in arranging programs.

By mandate in many states, all students must be scheduled for gym (dance) at least two periods each week. Despite this requirement, flexibility in the humanities curriculum can still be provided by arranging a staggered physical education program twice each week. Sixty or more students can be divided into three groups of 20 on the two gym days. Here, for example, would be a humanities class schedule that met on Tuesdays and Thursdays with group size ranging between 20 and 30 students:

Period 1 Group A students—in gym
      Group B students—with social studies
            teacher
      Group C students—with English teacher

Period 2 Group B students—in gym
      Group C students—with social studies
            teacher
      Group A students—with English teacher

Period 3 Group C students—in gym
      Group A students—with social studies
            teacher
      Group B students—with English teacher

The same pattern would be repeated for students in an afternoon humanities curriculum.

With this arrangement it is possible to have the English and social studies teachers combine their seminars for a large group session double period, or one teacher could take both seminar groups while the other meets with a single student or with a small group of students. Another pattern permits the English and social studies teachers to keep the same single seminar group of students together for a double period on Tuesday and then reverse the procedure on Thursday.

Only the gym teacher will find legitimate limitations to this flexible organization of a humanities curriculum. If the students are placed in three groups of 20 on the basis of social and academic rather than gymnastic skills, she will find it difficult to develop dance programs for the extremes of abilities in each gym class. She can also be expected to request that more than a single class period be made available for gym or dance twice each week.

Groupings can be altered and students can be given the option of choosing either dance or athletics for their gym period. Gym classes restructured to meet more than a single period on Tuesday or Thursday are also feasible alternatives. Seminar groups would then be arranged only after the students are given their gym class preferences. Here is how such an alternative schedule looks:

Tuesday:	Periods 1 & 2	Group A, Dance
		Group B, Social Studies
		Group C, English
	Period 3	Groups B & C, Gym
		1/2 group A, Social Studies
		1/2 group B, English
Thursday:	Periods 1 & 2	Groups B & C, Gym
		1/2 group A, Social Studies
		1/2 group A, English
	Period 3	Group A, Dance
		Group C, Social Studies
		Group B, English

As is evident, some of the seminar groups are now larger than others because dance sessions have to be smaller than physical education classes. Again teachers can switch classes to meet the needs of special programs. Probably the best solution to meeting legal requirements for gym classes and still retaining flexibility in scheduling a humanities curriculum is to organize physical education within a workshop program. (See chapter seven on workshop patterns.)

The Monday, Wednesday, Friday schedule when teachers in virtually all the disciplines are available provides great flexibility. Any number of interesting patterns can be used during the year to conform with educational needs. Some examples:

Monday   8:40 - 9:35 A.M.   All students attend lecture by visiting professor in auditorium.

          9:40 - 11:00 A.M.   Divide into three or four seminar groups for discussion. (English and social studies teacher plus one or more of resource staff— music, art, drama or dance teacher)

alternate: 8:40 - 10:05 A.M.   All students see and discuss film in auditorium.

          10:10 - 11:00 A.M.   Students report to resource teachers for project conferences.

alternate: 8:40 - 10:00 A.M.   Three seminar groups on book read by all students.

          10:05 - 11:00 A.M.   Independent study.

alternate: 8:40 - 11:00 A.M.   Students in various sections of the city working on projects previously approved.

A weekly schedule, developed by a joint student-faculty committee each week, would be distributed to all students in the humanities curriculum. The entire faculty would also receive copies. Here is a typical week program:

Hunter College High School

Humanities Curriculum (Public Man Theme)
Week of October 14 - 21

Monday, October 14th   A.M. & P.M. sessions—working in
                            school or city on individual projects
                            or at political campaign headquarters
                            in morning or afternoon.

Tuesday, October 15th   A.M.—Report at 8:40 A.M. to audito-
                            rium. Briefing on ballet program by
                            dance teacher. Attend Harkness Ballet
                            rehearsal at their studio until 11: 00.
                            P.M.—Groups A, B & C in two ses-
                            sion seminar on Machiavelli's *The
                            Prince* and gym class for one session.

Wednesday, October 16th   A.M.—Report at 8:40 to auditorium
                            for introductory lecture on Shake-
                            speare's *King Lear* by drama teacher.
                            10:00 A.M.—Small group discussions
                            on lecture.

                            P.M.—Introductory lecture on *King
                            Lear* at 11:45 in auditorium. A, B & C
                            group discussions on lecture at
                            1:45 P.M.

Thursday, October 17th   A.M.—8:40 A.M.—A, B & C seminar
                            sessions on Machiavelli's *The Prince*
                            and gym classes.

                            P.M.—Report to auditorium at 11:45
                            for briefing on ballet program by
                            dance teacher. Attend Harkness Ballet
                            rehearsal at their studio until
                            2:15 P.M.

Friday, October 18th   A.M. & P.M.—8:40 A.M. Report to
                            auditorium to hear introductory remarks
                            by music teacher on opera *Romeo and
                            Juliette*. 10:00 A.M.—All students
                            leave for Metropolitan Opera Company
                            rehearsal of *Romeo and Juliette*.

Sunday, October 20th 7:30 P.M.—All students attend preview of *King Lear* at Repertory Theater of Lincoln Center. Discussion following play with director and cast.

Students living in or near the large urban centers can tap the available cultural resources with little difficulty. That all too few school systems actually take advantage of their proximity to cultural centers is a strange and sad situation. Inertia and the absence of an adventuresome spirit are cruel school diseases.

When schools are too far removed from centers of culture substitute experiences are still available. For example, films, slides, television programs, poster displays, charts, records and photographs are easily borrowed from metropolitan museums and art studios. In most instances the only charge is postage. Again we find that such assistance is asked for all too infrequently.

MEETING WITH THE STUDENTS

After agreeing on forms and procedures, a humanities committee would meet with the eleventh grade students, the human guinea pigs for the humanities curriculum which would begin the following fall. Students will listen to the possible directions the faculty committee thinks the humanities curriculum might move. Suggestions from students are invited either at this initial meeting or later by submitting ideas on paper. Still later the students will decide whether they wish to elect the humanities curriculum for the equivalent of three Carnegie units of credit in English, social studies, and the arts or follow the regular program of senior courses in these subjects. In most schools the overwhelming majority of students can be expected to elect the humanities curriculum in the first trial year.

Selling the humanities curriculum to students who are itching for a change is not a difficult assignment. An old Irish proverb says, "You are easily led where you want to go." But a faculty will find that student in-put, after the first year, will involve far more than listening to what the faculty has decided and then making suggestions. Once the students' appetites for humanistic experiences have been whetted, they will demand the right to play a major role even in the initial thinking through of the curriculum design. As we shall see, when the teachers are willing to share decision-making, the total student commitment to the humanities curriculum is comparable to the spirit of a winning sports team.

THE IMPORTANCE OF THE INITIAL HUMANITIES SESSION

First impressions are of crucial importance both socially and educationally. No matter how dedicated the people or the program, if the initial meeting between students and teachers is neutral or stand-offish, the obstacles to the eventual success of any new school adventure are immeasurably increased. One's best educational foot needs to be put forward immediately. The students should have some perspective on what to anticipate in the humanities curriculum. But some element of pleasant surprise should also be planned. Instead of spending the first period talking about the humanities curriculum, a healthier procedure is to let the humanities speak for themselves.

In the first year of the Hunter humanities curriculum, the first day began by having all the students see a series of slides, first quickly and then a second time more slowly, of famous people from the past and present. For variety and humor, a few slides of our own students and teachers were thrown on the screen as well. The slides included paintings, sculpture, frescoes and photographs from Socrates to Pope John XXIII. Many were reproductions the students would see when they visited the museums during the school term. Film was also shown. A short clip of Stalin, another of Hitler, and Senator Edward Kennedy's eulogy of his brother Robert in St. Patrick's Cathedral. Finally, a comparison of Richard Nixon's "Checkers" speech on television in 1952 with the 1960 presidential debates.

We then asked, "What does this collage mean to you in relation to the first theme, The Public Man?" Students divided into seminar groups, a recorder was elected to summarize important points, and the fun of learning together was begun. On the second day, the recorders' comments served as a focus for further discussion. Despite the usual frustrations of a school—poor equipment, exterior noise, and interior heat—the first day proved to be an instant success.

Each time a new theme is introduced a new excitement needs to be generated. In the second year of the humanities curriculum, the initial theme was on the ancient Greeks. Both teachers and the secretarial staff combined their gastronomic talents to prepare Greek foods. Students were provided do-it-yourself recipes as well as an opportunity to taste delicious dishes almost fit for the Greek gods. And then the students were shown a modern film on the beauty of the ancient Greek world.

Having guest speakers who raise intriguing questions, going on special trips, showing slides and film, feeling, doing, tasting and participating in other activities, rather than having a simple recital of what will happen, are always stimulating introductions. Once the commitment is caught, the humanities curriculum will be in orbit.

CHAPTER 7

Lessons Learned in Launching
a Humanities Curriculum

School administrators and teachers willing to introduce a humanities curriculum must allow for many months of school meetings before the staff can be expected to reach basic agreements. Each school's humanities curriculum should be an indigenous product. The popular pattern of purchasing textbooks and having all the students read so many pages each day is to be avoided like the plague—and not just in a humanities curriculum!

When designing the curriculum outline around an understanding of men and events, one can easily fall into the trap of offering simplistic notions of black and white, of right and wrong. Students have been surfeited with the common clichés: that history never changes, as believed by some; that the world is evolving constantly for the better, from clan to tribe, to city, to state, to nation, to world government, as believed by others. Leaders should be examined,—people like Malcolm X, King Lear, Sir Thomas More, St. Joan, Socrates, and others to see if the dedicated or possessed are necessarily the most effective to take charge. Students should explore whether we really get whom we deserve as leaders.

A thematic organization in which four or five large topics serve as a unifying umbrella has proved an effective humanistic frame-work. In this design the separate disciplines can make their special contributions. "Man's Search for Identity" is probably one of the most popular central cultural approaches found in our schools. Because western civilization is far better known than the third world cultures, the majority of reading selections as well as art, music, and film experiences are steeped in the Judeo-Christian tradition and in the heritage of ancient Greece. We can anticipate that a better balance in emphasis will be found in humanistic studies once the current pro-western cultural bias is recognized and altered.

At Hunter in the program's first year, four themes were used—The Public Man, The Private Man, Man and Woman, and The Responsibilities of Man and Society. The Public Man theme capitalized on the national, state, and local elections which are always overriding issues in the mass media during the fall semester. Such diverse topics as the role of power, the urban environment, the nature of the public man, the influence of the arts and the mass media could be discussed. Poetry, literature, drama, film and philosophy can readily be brought to bear on The Public Man theme. For example, Shakespeare's *King Lear,* Plato's *Apology,* and Machiavelli's *The Prince* were some selections used. When *King Lear* was read in class, and later seen on the stage, the English teacher stressed its literary and dramatic qualities. But the play was also examined for the manner in which Shakespeare viewed power. Each of the four themes was explored for approximately a nine week period—The Public Man until the November elections, The Private Man until the end of January, Man and Woman in February and March, and the final theme, The Responsibilities of Man and Society, through June. Our hope and goal was that the last unit would result in a student affirmation for, rather than a rejection of society.

PROJECTS, GROUP AND INDIVIDUAL

To take students beyond the academic and into a self-realizing, creative experience, special projects were assigned for each of the four themes. As part of the first group project, all the students were asked to identify with a national or local candidate for political office and to provide active assistance in that individual's election. Time was allocated within the humanities schedule and after school for students to carry out this project. A note signed by the parent permitting the student to undertake the assignment, and another note from the campaign headquarters supervisor or political candidate accepting the student's services satisfied attendance requirements. Some students who could not stomach any of the candidates chose instead to undertake a sociological study of an election district. They then sought to predict how the people in the district would vote. Still others compared the current election techniques, particularly the use of television, with previous elections. One student selected several musical themes and created a eulogy to John F. Kennedy.

Making a mini Greek vase after visiting the local museum and attending a lecture-demonstration on Greek civilization was another group project. Everyone participated. The students were given a small bag of clay and were told to go home and design their own "Greek" vases. Some of the results were so fine that the museum authorities made a display and took photographs for their magazine. Virtually all the students enjoyed the experience of working with their hands as well as their minds. A third group project undertaken as part of The Public Man theme proved equally exciting. All students were asked to take photographs or make sketches of any building in the community that demonstrated a Greek architectural style. Another year, virtually all the students enjoyed and profited by making colorful heraldic banners in conjunction with the Renaissance theme. Placing them on display in the school halls gave a new, exciting tone to the building.

Projects took two forms: the group work completed by all students as described above, and four individual projects related again to each of the four themes. Students were required to use a different discipline to express their ideas each time they moved to a new area of study. Thus a student who concentrated in the field of music for the first theme, The Public Man, might elect art or dance or history or architecture as the primary discipline for her individual project when dealing with the second theme, The Private Man. Usually one of the humanities teaching team served as advisor. On occasion other teachers with special competencies agreed to help several students.

In general, the group projects in which everyone participated caused no major problems. A different situation emerged with the individual projects. When the idea of project rotation to a new discipline for each of the four themes was announced, a considerable number of students voiced strenuous opposition. They preferred to work on individual projects in those disciplines with which they were most comfortable. "Why should we move into the field of art when we enjoy staying with the history teacher?" some students protested. (Students are always more willing to radicalize society than themselves.) We insisted. Our view was that students should taste each of the disciplines even if the experience was not one of instant success. Exposure to a variety of creative activities would sensitize students to the difficulties as well as the special skills involved. We wanted students to understand how a painter, a composer, a sculptor, or an anthropologist uses his tools, how he thinks, and hopefully why he creates as he does. And we believed that by immersing oneself in a new discipline each time the class started a new theme these questions could be faced intelligently. That the student did not succeed in becoming another Picasso, Stravinsky, or Edward Durrell Stone bothered the faculty not at all. But for students this new understanding of what constituted achievement in a humanities curriculum took time to accept.

The student whose musical eulogy of President Kennedy received tremendous applause when played on tape for all the students had been particularly vehement in opposing the idea of four different project disciplines. She was most at home with literature and wished only to do "her own thing." Agreement to use music as her initial theme came only with the greatest reluctance and only after she accepted the fact that the literature teacher had no more time for additional students. After the tape was played she was asked, "Did you feel like a manipulator putting all those tapes of music together?" Her answer: "I felt wonderful—like a musical composer—and I can't wait to try other ideas."

We insisted because a humanities curriculum, like life, must be felt. A major problem with the overwhelming majority of current humanities courses is that they are only intellectualized. It is not enough to read a poem or a book, see a film, or go on an architectural tour of the city. Students need to taste and feel the pain and joy of writing their own poems, preparing their own films, and planning their own environment for living. Young people particularly live in a sensual world. Marshall McLuhan's message on the impact of the mass media is not an idle boast. Although the printed word will not soon become extinct, the utilization of the mass media for learning is one of the principal neglected areas in our schools today.

Of course it is essential that students be aware of their heritage. An important level of understanding and feeling is reached when we comprehend what others have done; a different and often deeper level is achieved when we become the creators. The level of involvement assumes a qualitative rather than a quantitative dimension.

We insisted on different disciplines being attempted for each of the four themes for practical reasons as well. No teacher should be burdened with too many individual student projects. By asking the students to choose different disciplines for individual projects each time a new theme was begun, all teachers could be assigned a fair share of the total student load. For example, if 80 students were involved in the morning humanities curriculum, five teachers on the staff—English, social studies, music, art and drama—would each serve as advisors for 16 students. But when would students find the time to undertake the individual projects and still keep up with all the work required for the humanities seminar sessions? When would the faculty find the time to meet with students to discuss their projects? Our initial solution to these problems during the first year of the experiment was to call an abrupt halt to group seminar sessions from time to time. By doing so students were able to meet with their advisors during the school day as well as to complete their individual projects. During The Public Man theme students were released for a full week from "regular" humanities classes. For the second theme we tried a different approach. One day each week was set aside as free time for individual project work.

Free time proved to be too simplistic a solution. In what can only be interpreted as a sad commentary on how poorly we prepare students to handle freedom, the students complained about the liabilities of too much unscheduled time. When they knew that a full week or two of freedom was available for individual projects, the tendency all too often was to idle away the time until the last day and then to work like slaves. Under such circumstances individual projects become less than a joyous, creative opportunity. Surely the need to offer students genuine opportunities for the exercise of freedom with responsibility in a democratic society must begin earlier than the senior year of high school!

A better plan was needed to harmonize the realities of time limitations, the availability of teachers, and the need for students to have a wide choice of creative experiences with individual projects. The answer: incorporate the individual projects in workshop sessions scheduled for the first hour each day in the A.M. and P.M. humanities curriculum. By channeling individual projects within a workshop framework all students wishing to work in the same discipline could be scheduled together with a skilled teacher at the same time every day. Whenever the workshop teachers and students need additional time, the humanities seminar classes meeting the second and third hours could be cancelled and the workshop sessions extended. A reciprocal arrangement is possible if seminar sessions need more hours for guest speakers, a film, trips, etc. Faculty cooperation makes it possible for workshop or seminar teachers to cover one another's classes if an extended humanities session is scheduled. Levels of teacher understanding and appreciation can be expected to rise immeasurably when an English teacher, for example, spends a period working with, or learning with students in a music or art class while their teacher holds forth in a humanities program. And it is healthy for students to see their English teacher in a new relationship away from her English classroom home base. Here is one typical student's program with the workshop structure:

A.M. Humanities

Period	Monday	Tuesday	Wednesday	Thursday	Friday
1	Workshop*	Workshop*	Workshop*	Workshop*	Workshop*
2 3	Humanities Seminar	Humanities Seminar	Humanities Seminar	Humanities Seminar	Humanities Seminar

Period	Monday	Tuesday	Wednesday	Thursday	Friday
4			LUNCH		
		OFFICIAL (HOME) ROOM			
5	Spanish	Free	Spanish	Spanish	Spanish
6	English Elective	English Elective	English Elective	English Elective	English Elective
7 8	Science Elective	Science Elective	Science Elective	Science Elective	Science Elective

*In art, photography, music, literature, anthropology, dance, etc., depending on availability of teachers and student interest.

The P.M. humanities students would follow a similar schedule with the workshop held on the fifth period each day and the seminars periods six and seven. By scheduling the workshop the first period in the humanities curriculum, the students have a skilled advisor readily available for assistance; they can associate with other students interested in the same discipline, and they still could feel free to express themselves in their discipline choice and allocate time for creative work. Students should be given the opportunity to select their workshop preferences. If a student's first workshop choice must be denied because of space limitiations for one theme unit, she can be given high priority when assigning workshops for the next theme.

Here is a sample letter that could be mailed to the students during the summer months:

> Even though September seems light-years away, the humanities staff wants to welcome you now to the program.
>
> We have two things in mind:
>
> 1. Two *required* books for summer reading: Camus' *The Plague* and Homer's *Iliad* (Penguin Classics edition, please). We will begin with these two books the first weeks in September. As you read carefully, you might ask yourself why we paired them. What do they say about the changing spirit of man and the world in which he acts?

We *suggest* that those of you who are in the city this summer go to see the stunning exhibition of art from Africa and Oceania at the Metropolitan Museum of Art (free on Mondays, open til 10 P.M. on Tuesdays) and any or all of the Shakespeare-in-the-parks.

2. Previews of coming attractions: the student representatives that you elected met with us on June 26th. From their suggestions and our thinking, we've planned a program.

This year's humanities curriculum will explore the humanistic spirit in various literary, historical and artistic contexts, in the past and in our own times.

New things this year will include:

a) a new overall organization
b) new cultural experiences inside and outside of school
c) many different "great works" to read and discuss in depth in small-group seminars, and
d) a daily workshop program which will permit you to elect during the year as many as four different areas of creative concentration. (Well, not quite four—physical education is mandated in our state, but you can choose when you want to take it.)

Each humanities teacher has listed the workshops which he or she will offer in the course of the year. We are asking you now to read this mini catalogue carefully, to try to think of the year as a whole, but elect *now* your first, second and third choices for the first quarter's workshop, and return the enclosed postcard to us *before* August 10th. We'll try to give you your first choice, but if you don't get it this time, you probably will the next. Sorry, but if we don't hear from you by the 10th, we'll have to schedule you ourselves to balance out group sizes. You have been scheduled for either the A.M. or P.M. humanities because of your three electives outside the program; therefore, you *must* choose from those workshops which are in your time slot as indicated at the top of page one of this letter.

A suggestion—keep this catalogue for future reference. Our school has a habit of running out of paper.

We hope you're having a marvelous summer (while we're here slaving over a hot humanities!).

See you in September.

Our best wishes,
The Humanities Staff

Students in a workshop would remain together with the same

teacher for an entire nine week period. All the humanities students would then be regrouped completely when new workshop choices are made for the next theme. They would then find themselves with a new teacher, a new discipline, and new students. For example, if 16 students are registered for music during the first nine week theme, The Public Man, all of them would move along to one of the other disciplines for the second theme, The Private Man. Perhaps five would elect art, three would go to drama, six to literature, etc. And each teacher would meet a totally new student mix at the conclusion of each nine week cycle.

Nearly always the workshops would be informal, relaxed sessions. Sometimes the teacher could ask all the students to meet together for some generalized discussion, to give advice, or to share in the accomplishment of a workshop member. More often the teacher would be seen working individually with a student. On occasion students would not report to the workshop at all but might pursue their tasks in another part of the school or in the community. With a workshop pattern both teacher and student could meet as needed. Both would be aware of the goal and the progress of individual projects. Time should always be provided at the conclusion of each theme to have all students share in what each workshop has accomplished. An art show, a drama presentation, a musical performance, readings, etc., would be scheduled for the last phase of each theme. Here is an example of how a workshop program can be organized.

I. *Workshops in the FIRST QUARTER (5th Century Athens) will include:* (9 weeks)

Morning Session

A. Social Studies—Mr. Slauson
City Politics: A study of how cities are governed, with an introductory overview of ancient Athens and a major emphasis on contemporary New York City. The workshop will also stress an analysis of and an involvement in the current New York elections.

B. Drama—Miss Balf
In all four quarters of the Dramatic Workshop, original

improvisations of the students will be used to teach the following acting techniques and skills:

> the strengthening of the student's "observation" and "recall"
>
> the development of acute sense perceptions
>
> how to build character (motivation, drives, goals, selectivity of actions, use of imagination, stage business, etc.)
>
> how to build a scene (timing, conflict, dramatic build, climax)
>
> use of stage (placement, blocking, stage movement, entrances, exits)

Also, we are planning supplementary reading of plays with periodic discussions—and voluntary playwriting for students who want it, plus possible performance in the workshop.

In addition, in each quarter, wherever possible, we will endeavor to apply the techniques studied by attempting to perform a scene (or scenes) relevant to the period under discussion.

First Quarter: Scene from the Greek Theatre

C. English—Mrs. Laster
Greek Tragedy—Readings of several tragedies by Aeschylus, Sophocles and Euripides to explore the nature of tragedy as well as the context in which these plays were created.

D. Music Workshop—Mr. Kaplan
The role of music in classical and modern cultures. Balance, mimesis and theatrical derivations; disorder; urbanization and confrontation; "pop" culture; art and technology.

E. Dance—Mrs. Condon
The Dance workshop will provide for students the means to develop dance technique and to create original dance studies based on various art forms of dance and myth. These workshops will enable students to express feelings and ideas through rhythms, muscular dynamics and spatial arrangements.

Workshop in Greek myth will include—
1. Dance technique (modern and/or ballet)
2. An original dance study based on a dramatic moment or crucial episode from Greek mythology. (This original dance may be an individual or group study.)

Course requirements: black leotard and tights, ballet slippers, notebook. Little or no previous dance experience necessary.

There is no such thing as authentic Greek dance. Dancers have long been intrigued by sculpture, ceramics and mythology, and dances have been created in both modern and ballet styles based on the Greek art and myth.

Afternoon Session

A. Social Studies—Mrs. Greenspan
An Introduction to Cultural Anthropology—A study of pre-industrial societies through myth, language, religion and social and political institutions.

B. Sculpture Workshop—Miss Rosso
A study of third dimensional concepts of space in contemporary sculpture and in outstanding individual works of the past. Media: clay, plaster, new materials. Pottery as sculpture will also be included.

C. English—Mr. Baratta
See A.M. Schedule

D. Dance—Mrs. Condon
See A.M. Schedule

II.*Workshops in SECOND QUARTER (Renaissance) will include:* (9 weeks)

Morning Session

A. Social Studies—Mr. Slauson
Elizabethan England: A political, cultural and religious analysis of Tudor England, centering around the person of the Queen and the problems of an emerging "great society." Students may choose individual areas of interest.

B. Photography—Miss Rosso
Study of outstanding photos of the past, with emphasis on the development of skills and techniques necessary for picture taking and printing in black and white. Use of a camera as a creative tool for personal expression.

C. English—Mrs. Laster
Non-Shakespearean Elizabethan Drama—Workshop in the plays of Shakespeare's contemporaries—Marlowe, Webster, and Tourneur—to examine the creative spirit of the age that witnessed the highest achievement in the English theatre.

D. Dance—Mrs. Condon
Pre-Classic dance forms will include:

1. Modern dance technique
2. Pre-Classical dance forms. (Original dance composition from a historical and musical approach.) Studies will include the Pavan, Galliard, Courante, Gigue, and Minuet.

Course requirements: black leotard and tights, notebook.
Text: Horst, Louis: *Pre-Classic Dance Forms,* Dover ($1.00 paperback—to be purchased in school). Some experience in dance technique and music appreciation.

Afternoon Session

A. Social Studies—Mrs. Greenspan
Comparative Religion: Readings in the great literature of five of the world's "great" religions: Judaism, Christianity, Islam, Buddhism, Hinduism.

B. Drama—Miss Balf
Commedia del Arte improvisations

C. English—Mr. Baratta
See A.M. Schedule

D. Music—Mr. Kaplan
20th Century as a neo-Renaissance movement—the new consciousness. Study of and experimentation with 14th, 15th, 16th and 20th century forms including multi-media art (film animation and anti-art); religious, secular and avant-garde music; Renaissance humanism and modern individualism.

E. Dance—Mrs. Condon
See A.M. Schedule

III. *Workshops in the THIRD QUARTER (Early 20th Century) will include:* (6 weeks)

Morning Session

A. Dance—Mrs. Condon
Workshop in the Ballet will include:

> 1. Classical ballet technique
> 2. Appreciation of the ballet
>   a. visits to ballet schools
>   b. attending one concert on the ballet

Course requirement: black leotard and tights, ballet slippers, white nylon anklets. No experience necessary.

B. Drama—Miss Balf
Scene from early 20th century theatre; and, if the group is large enough and so desires, a possible scene from Restoration comedy as a dramatic contrast.

C. Literature—Mrs. Laster
Workshop in creative writing. Each member will pursue several writing projects in fiction, poetry, or drama. In addition, the group will study the early works of one or two writers as an indication of how accomplished artists have dealt with the problems of their first writing.

D. Graphics—Miss Rosso
Graphics as a fine art will be explored. New printing techniques using woodcuts, serigraph, cardboard and linoleum. Study of social significance of prints of the past and examination and critique of 20th century posters.

E. Social Studies—Mrs. Greenspan
An Introduction to Freudian Psychology: Basic psychoanalytic theory explored through selections from Freud's writings.

Afternoon Session

A. Dance Workshop—Mrs. Condon
See A.M. Schedule

B. Literature—Mr. Baratta
Creative Writing: a consideration of several theories and techniques of literary composition with readings in the critical writings of Arnold, Wordsworth, Sydney, Caudwell, Frye and others. The focus will be on the students' own writings.

C. Music Workshop—Mr. Kaplan
Analysis—creation—experimentation with 20th century derivations: impressionism, neo-classicism, nationalism, atonality, origins of the avant-garde, and related abstract and expressionist movements.

D. Photography—Miss Rosso

E. Social Studies—Mr. Slauson
Pre-contemporary Europe: a slice of European history from about 1880 to 1914 or 1919 with stress on social and cultural aspects. We shall focus on the attacks on and apparent breakdown of the 19th century's tradition of liberalism and progress. Readings will be in literature and social sciences as well as in "straight history." Some attention will be given to art and music.

IV. *Workshops in the FOURTH QUARTER (Modern Times) will include:* (12 weeks)

Morning Session

A. Dance—Mrs. Condon
Workshop in Modern Dance Technique and Modern Forms will include:
   1. Modern Dance Technique (Graham)
   2. Modern Forms Composition (Original Dance Compositions)
      a. Introspection—Expressionism
      b. Cerebralism
      c. Jazz
      d. Americana
      e. Impressionism

Course requirements: black leotard and tights, notebook. No experience necessary.

B. Literature—Mrs. Laster
The workshop will read a number of short works by a group of 20th century writers—Conrad, James, Mann, Kafka, Gide, Sartre, Beckett—who have influenced the shape and direction of modern writing and thought.

C. Music—Mr. Kaplan
The construction of a multi-media environmental work:

Violence in Society as perceived, interpreted and expressed through sound and film.

D. Painting Workshop—Miss Rosso
An analysis of painting of the 20th century dealing with new concepts of "What is Art," new techniques, new materials, with emphasis on students' own creative work.

E. Social Studies—Mrs. Greenspan
Contemporary philosophy: readings in Marxism, existentialism, objectivism, philosophy of the cruel.

Afternoon Session

A. Dance—Mrs. Condon
See A.M. Schedule

B. Drama—Miss Balf
   1. Improvisations in 20th century styles: romantic, realistic, naturalistic, expressionistic, "Theatre of the Absurd."
   2. Scene from a "Theatre of the Absurd" play and possibly from the "Theatre of Cruelty."

C. Literature—Mr. Baratta
Goethe's *Faust:* the foundation of the modern imagination.

D. Social Studies—Mr. Slauson
Revolutionary societies at home and abroad: continuing depth studies of today's China, Cuba and revolutionary-minded communities in the U.S. Emphasis will be on individual study and on the relationship of theory to practice.

SEMINAR SESSIONS

The workshops are designed to provide students with opportunities to select a special discipline for indepth work throughout a theme unit. The seminars give all students common learning experiences in readings, trips, films, and guests. Where possible, the activities of each workshop are related to the central theme emphasized in the seminars. The workshops can be seen as the creative, personal, action expression; the seminar as the cerebral and visceral experience.

In class scheduling, there are such opposite situations as too little and too much flexibility. A humanities curriculum should be geared to flexibility. By having an entire morning or an entire afternoon in which to organize learning experiences, an almost limitless number of class combinations and time allotments become possible. But an element of stability also has a legitimate place in school and life. When devising a humanities curriculum, or anything else, the aim should be to offer sufficient variety to keep everyone interested and, at the same time, sufficient regularity to keep everyone going.

Changing the seminar schedule each day—different teachers, different rooms, different times—after the first flush of excitement, causes too much confusion and instability for both students and teachers. Constant change in the first year of the humanities curriculum provided variety. It also caused chaos. A weekly program was printed every Friday, following the student-faculty planning sessions, detailing where students and teachers would meet on the succeeding week. But a program schedule is not enough. For example, it becomes almost impossible for students to sense any continuity in discussions when on Monday, the English teacher meets with them, on Wednesday, the social studies teacher, and on Friday, the drama teacher, to examine the same book or film. To follow so changeable a schedule would require that the humanities faculty confer with each other and compare notes each day—a requirement high school teachers, who have responsibilities to teach other classes as well, cannot fulfill. Under such circumstances, students and teachers came to the conclusion that the first year's humanities curriculum was *too* flexible.

A better pattern of scheduling the seminar sessions was devised for the program's second year. In contrast with the workshops where students choose their personal preferences, the students were arranged alphabetically for the initial seminars. These students, approximately 20 in each group, would remain with the same teacher for a two or three week period as they discussed a single book. At the conclusion of the work, the twenty students would move along to a second humanities teacher for a two or three week discussion period dealing with a new book. When the first theme, fifth century Athens, was replaced with the next unit, The Renaissance, all seminar students would be regrouped into new divisions of 20 for the second nine week theme. Here is how a student's schedule might be arranged for the first three themes from September through March:

First Theme—The Public Man or Fifth Century Athens

Period 1—Four Workshops—15 students in each—English, history, drama and art teachers.

Period 2   60 students divided into three seminars with instruc-
and   tors changed approximately every three weeks.
Period 3   English teacher—20 students
                History teacher—20 students
                Drama teacher —20 students

Second Theme—The Private Man or the Renaissance

Period 1—Four Workshops—15 students each—photography, psychology, literature and music teachers.

Period 2   60 students differently grouped in three seminars from
and   first theme.
Period 3   Drama teacher —20 students
                History teacher—20 students
                English teacher—20 students

Third Theme—Man And Woman or Early Twentieth Century

Period 1—Four Workshops—15 students each—dance, film, history and anthropology.

Period 2   60 students again reorganized in three seminars for new
and   theme.
Period 3   English teacher—20 students
                History teacher—20 students
                Music teacher —20 students

By the time a theme unit is completed in nine or ten weeks, each student seminar group will have worked at least once with each of the three seminar teachers. Having the same teacher meet with the same students on a single book results in a deeper sense of continuity, understanding and interaction for both students and teachers.

Student seminars and workshops are of course nothing new. But when related to four thematic units, when undertaken in a different discipline each time, when inner satisfaction and pride are substituted for grades and extra credits, when they appeal to the visual, to the tactile, to the senses rather than just to the traditionally academic, then seminars and workshops do constitute a new dimension in a student's approach to a special assignment. The more responsibility based on reason and understanding we offer youngsters, the more they will rise to the challenge. The more we differentiate learning and give wider scope to what is meant by achievement, the more a school program becomes worth doing. Humanities seminars and workshops provide such opportunities.

THE SERVICE PROJECT

Our most successful and most troubling project reports occurred with the final theme, The Responsibilities of Man and Society. The following information sheet was distributed to all students.

Dear Student:

Here is the information you will need before deciding on your project The Responsibilities of Man and Society. Remember, please, that our goal is to take an affirmative action, to consider others, and to give of ourselves. In some tangible way we wish to serve a segment of humanity. In the process we may be "servicing" ourselves. Fine. Whether you work individually or in a group, whether you spend your time and demonstrate your talents in a ghetto school, the medical examiner's office, city hall, a hospital, a welfare office, a narcotic center, or with a single child—we ask you to follow this procedure:

1. Discuss your project proposal with a teacher in the humanities program.
2. Complete the attached form, making certain all adults have signed as indicated.

Where possible, the morning humanities students will work on their projects Monday, Wednesday and Friday mornings. Humanities classes will be held in the school on Tuesdays and Thursdays. The afternoon humanities students will follow a similar schedule in their afternoon sessions each week.

Each student will receive a time sheet which will be signed by the supervisor of the service project outside of school. The time sheet, similar to the form used by college student teachers, will be filed on the last school day in May, and again on June 26th.

Students in the morning program may have more difficulty in locating a suitable place to render service during the early hours of the day. If a student develops a service project that requires additional hours on Monday, Wednesday and Friday, special arrangements can be made *if* the project is approved and the time away from school does not interfere with classes or commitments in the school that have a higher priority. Students who desire more time for service projects than will be granted all students *must* receive special permission from the humanities staff. The service projects will begin officially on Monday, May 19th following the Advanced Placement examinations and will conclude with student reports on June 26th and June 27th. We hope you will select areas of work which will prove to be both stimulating and fun. Your contribution to others will be successful if you have helped other people experience some added enjoyment and meaning in living as a human being. Good luck!

Hunter College High School
Humanities Curriculum

Fourth Theme: The Responsibilities of Man and Society
Service Project: May 19th–June 27th

Name:_____Class:_____

Description of Service: (include location, days, time and name of supervisor)

I have interviewed the student listed above and I approve having her contribute her services to this organization.

Service Project:_____
Signature of Supervisor:_____
Address:_____

_____

I approve my daughter's absence from school in order to fulfill the requirements of her service as described above.

Signature of Parent:_____

_____

I approve the service project for the fourth theme.

Signature of Teacher:_____

Special Considerations:

When the completed form is returned, the students would be given the following:

Dear_____

Your service project proposal has been approved by the student-faculty committee. We are attaching a time sheet which your supervisor is to sign each day you are at work. If you are ill on one of your service days (Monday, Wednesday, Friday) and are unable to report to your supervisor, we ask that you telephone Mr. Lee, our attendance officer, (360-2539) and your official attendance record will then be consistent with the time sheet. All time sheets will be filed with Mrs. Caloritis on Monday, June 26th.

One or more of the teachers on the humanities staff will visit you at your service project and confer with your supervisor. As you know, all the students will meet on the mornings of June 26 and June 27 to comment on their projects and to evaluate the program.

We will continue to have guest speakers each Tuesday and Thursday on the theme The Responsibilities of Man and Society. The final book we shall read and discuss in the humanities curriculum will be Charles Frankel's *The Case for Modern Man,* (Beacon Press Paperback, Boston, 1955), available in your library as well as at school. If you have any further questions about the procedure to be followed, get in touch immediately with one of the teachers in the humanities program. We hope your service project proves to be another valuable experience for you now and in the future.

Sincerely,

Humanities Staff

Humanities Curriculum
Fourth Theme: The Responsibilities of Man and Society

May-June

Service Project Location:_____

Service Project Supervisor:_____

Date	Time on Project	Signature of Supervisor

* * * * * *

To the classroom teacher:

Dear_____:

_____ has submitted a special service project which will necessitate her absence from your class on Monday, Wednesday and Friday. Her project supervisor has indicated that she cannot adequately fulfill the project requirements in the regular time allotted to the students. A brief statement of her project is listed below. All the teachers in the humanities program have reviewed her request and agree that it merits making an exception to the regular time requirements. Teachers in the humanities program will visit all students at their service projects and confer with the supervisor.

A faculty evaluation session in which we hope you will participate will be held at 2:15 P.M. on Wednesday, June 4 in room 205.

Again, our thanks to you for your cooperation.

Project:

Sincerely,
Humanities Staff

In developing the fourth theme to include a service project we wished to incorporate the best features of the senior seminar program with the unit on The Responsibilities of Man and Society. Moving the final projects outside the pattern of the three previous themes would we hoped rekindle student interest, would provide a needed community service, and would conclude the humanities curriculum on a high note of achievement.

Most of the students who chose to work in ghetto schools and in other service areas for three days each week came back with glowing reports. Many wished they could have begun such service sooner. Some students stayed in school and served as teacher assistants. One student who, for personal reasons, refused to undertake a service project was permitted to stay in the school library or attend other classes. We received wonderful reports from the supervisors about the contributions and value of the experiment to the community.

But the absence of the seniors from the building for three days out of five made a difference for the rest of the students. The senior class assumes many leadership responsibilities in the operation of a school newspaper and allied publications, general office organization and administration, clubs, and other school activities which are of crucial importance for the entire student body. The sudden exodus of the seniors had not been thought through and essential meetings in school tended to become unstrung during the period of the final project.

A second mistake was made when the service projects were announced. In the initial statement to the students the following sentences were included:

> If a student develops a service project that requires additional hours on Monday, Wednesday, and Friday, special arrangements can be made if the project is approved and the time away from school does not interfere with regents' classes or other classes or commitments in the school that have a higher priority. Students who desire more time for service projects than will be granted all students *must* receive special permission from the humanities staff.

This clear statement turned out to be an albatross around the necks of the humanities staff. Invariably students found service opportunities that could only be fulfilled by being available five days each week. At the very least the special permission was for an entire school day on the three days officially granted for service projects.

What happened? The humanities staff refused to grant special permission if other teachers who met regularly with the students in non-humanities courses failed to give their consent. But these teachers protested that the onus of blame for refusal to give students special opportunities was arbitrarily shifted to them! The teachers, with good reason, felt that attendance in their classes was just as important as attendance at some humanistic service project. We have here still another example of how the road to hell is paved with good intentions. Again the humanities staff learned a profitable, but bitter lesson. During the second year of the program the service project was begun far sooner than mid-May. The final unit began immediately following the spring recess in late March thereby providing the students with a larger period of time—more than two months—in which to work in their service project. But now the service projects were scheduled for just twice each week and under *no* conditions could students ask for additional time that would interfere with other school commitments. Once these ground rules were clearly understood the students found little difficulty in finding service projects that conformed with the new time schedule. We would recommend that schools desiring to involve students in a service project as part of the humanities curriculum follow a similar procedure.

In the final unit a student's schedule would take this form:

Fourth Theme: The Responsibilities of Man and Society

Mon., April 27	Project Day. A.M. and P.M. Students in humanities curriculum working either in school or community for an entire morning or afternoon session.
Tues., April 28	Period 1—Workshops—elected by students—in photography, ceramics, dance, etc. Periods 2 & 3—Study groups—a different grouping of students from workshops. Selected areas offered based on student interest: black

	history, religion, existentialism, modern poetry, etc.
Wed., April 29	Project Day. A.M. and P.M.
Thurs., April 30	Period 1—Workshops Periods 2 & 3—Large group session: speaker on modern architecture.

The Friday schedule generally involved a combined session with all groups for the double period following the workshops. Special films were shown on this day to all humanities students, as well as group tours of local art galleries, music programs, etc. When workshop classes needed additional time, the study group sessions could be shortened and the workshop groups could continue their activities. As can be seen above, workshops and study groups were scheduled for three days each week, and service projects on Monday and Wednesday.

We have in this format flexibility within a definite structure. By placing the responsibility for the exact division of time on those most directly involved—the humanities team and the students, an administrator can open the school schedule to one that is educationally rather than just administratively viable. Not everyone will be satisfied. But while respecting the right of minority opinion to want no structure at all, or on the other hand, far tighter structure, the vast majority of teachers and students will thrive in this new climate of creative thinking about the use of time during the school day. Changing the pace and pattern of school life is guaranteed to remove the boredom and bitterness that infects our institutions. Try it. Schools have nothing to lose but their regularity.

THE PROBLEMS AND JOYS OF GUESTS

Guests are always unpredictable. Virtually every person requested as a speaker or resource can be expected to accept even though no honorarium or even train fare can be offered. Most will feel honored to be asked. A school will be fortunate if appropriate adults can be found for each theme. But be prepared for some surprises once a guest arrives. Often the speakers will ramble on and on even though they are asked to be brief and to leave plenty of time for questions. In some instances the guests will not be well prepared; sometimes they are so well prepared that they tell the students everything. Nothing is left for the imagination, nor is there any inducement for students to dig deeper. The temptation to pontificate before a captive audience is too great an opportunity to resist for some important people.

Nevertheless, it is essential that students have opportunities to hear a new voice, and see new faces in the school. Most of the guests will prove welcome additions, but even if the regular teacher could explain a situation or an idea better than the guest, other gains are registered when variety is added to the program. If nothing else, a boring guest will make the students reappraise their teacher with new respect. Certainly the change from a one-teacher monopoly with students to a proliferation of "teachers," many with conflicting views, is a healthy base for learning. From time to time, students themselves should serve as guest speakers when they have special competencies on a specific topic. Often, students will be more understanding, and tolerant, and attentive to their peers than to older guests. Using guests and students as teachers to augment learning is another much neglected resource in our schools and communities. And here is another way in which a humanities curriculum can make a healthy difference in a school program.

THEATRE, OPERA, FILM, SYMPHONY

Urban dwellers are supposed to be sophisticated individuals because so much culture is always available. Actually their provincialism is astounding. Many visitors to New York have seen more of its great attractions than the natives. Lincoln Center, for example, with its bounty of opera, theatre, symphonic orchestras, ballet and the other performing arts is a place many New York City students have never explored or experienced. For urban, suburban, and rural students, the performing arts should be a basic ingredient in their humanities curriculum. For both spectators and participants, sessions need to be specifically designed to expose the students to the best examples of man's interpretations of life in the arts.

One cannot overemphasize the importance of having attendance at art presentations become an active, personal experience. Negative judgments about classical music, ballet, Shakespeare, and the modern electronic and spontaneous arts are much simpler to make and defend when nothing is really known. Students must come to these presentations with questions. They must be willing to let the drama or the movement speak its special language. They must be given every opportunity to meet the human beings responsible for the creative development and execution of the art they are watching and hopefully feeling and understanding.

If a humanities program is fortunate, the play or film attended will be scheduled at a time when the theme of the production coincides with the current theme of the humanities curriculum. Shakespeare's *King Lear* and the film *The Lion in Winter,* for example, offered excellent leads for The Public Man theme. Sometimes, when free tickets are available, students will attend an opera or orchestra rehearsal even though the program is not directly germane to the immediate work. For example, we would have preferred to take the students to the Gounod opera *Romeo et Juliette* when we dealt with the theme Man and Woman but the Metropolitan Opera does not set its schedule on the needs of a school humanities curriculum.

Prior to every performance students attend, the music or drama teacher should provide background information and raise questions everyone should consider as they watch and hear the program. At most theatre presentations, the director can be prevailed upon to meet with the students and answer questions. On several occasions it is also possible to meet the leading actors after the performance. Such a procedure adds greatly to the thrill of the theatrical experience. And the city becomes the school. Time must also be permitted to have a further discussion for at least some minutes on the next day in school.

MUSEUM VISITS

One of the permanent benefits of the humanities curriculum on the total school atmosphere is the fresh outlook with which the staff and the students "discover" the museums of the city. For most students a museum trip means only a chance to get away from the classroom routine. They walk a great deal, hear more miscellaneous information about more paintings or artifacts than can possibly be remembered, and return home with sore feet. Such a barrage approach to museum visits may have some merit. But a museum can serve as a more meaningful experience if the trip is specific, concentrated, and coordinated. Several of the humanities students came to consider the Metropolitan Museum of Art as a second home. Worthwhile procedures were followed each time a visit was scheduled. An art teacher or a museum lecturer would show slides in the school and explain some of the special features for the students to examine when they saw the actual paintings the following day at the museum. Often the program began by asking the students what they saw in the paintings, why the museum might have purchased them, and similar questions.

Our greatest "triumph" came when several students in the art workshop developed their own tour guide for all the humanities students to follow. Students who had visited the museum several times to make selections and outline a route, distributed maps and suggestions to the others. These students then placed themselves in strategic positions at the museum and were ready to answer questions as their colleagues strolled by. Young people object strenuously to being herded around a museum—or anyplace else. With the student guides, all students could move from one painting to the next at their own pace and stay as long as they wished to examine a particular exhibit. "Nobody was teaching us," said the students. "We did it on our own. We are afraid to ask a lecturer questions partly because we do not wish to reveal our ignorance before everyone in a large group. But with this arrangement we are less hesitant to ask. And if the student guide doesn't know, she asks for us all." So successful were the senior students with their tour of renaissance art, for example, that when the tenth grade social studies classes discussed this historical period in class, the "senior experts" conducted the sophomores through the Metropolitan Museum of Art.

Here are some examples of student-devised guides to the museum. In style and in emphasis they illustrate how students will sometimes relate and reach one another in ways adults cannot duplicate:

We hope you enjoy this crazy tour. It shouldn't take more

than 15 minutes. This tour was designed so that you could carefully look at each piece and not be rushed on by some scatterbrained guide. It isn't a matter of life and death that you look at everything that is described here; these are just the things that we thought you might find interesting. Well, here goes nothin'.

When you enter the museum you will see the main stairway. Go to the hall to the left of the stairway. You will see an escalator. Do not go up, but look at the gigantic head next to it. This is Constantine. We all know who he is, right? Now go to the opposite side of the hall and look at a small sculpture. It is supposed to represent Jonah and the whale in two parts. Jonah is being swallowed on the right and spewed from the whale on the left. Some whale isn't it? It looks like a serpent with teeth. Next to it is some gold jewelry. Above it is a mosaic of the Lamb of God. Note the gold background and the black outlines. Next to the jewelry is a case of enamels. Note the similarity between the mosaics and the enamels. The people in them all tend to have blank expressions on their faces and they both tend to be cartoon-like. Next to the enamels is a bust of a lady of rank. She is clutching something like it's her last hope. It has a kind of classic simplicity.

Directly across from this lady is another lady. She's standing on the right of the top shelf. Look at her and some bronze statues always noting the classic simplicity and the Oriental decoration and then go back across the hall to a fragment of a marble sarcophagus. You will recognize it because at first glance it appears to be a man suffering from severe nausea but it's supposed to represent the deceased reading a scroll.

Go back across the hall to a group of hanging lamps. There is a griffin (who looks like your mother sometimes looks when you come in three hours late), a ridiculous foot, a bear that looks like a dog, a peacock and a lamp with running dog finials. You'll see what those are when you get there.

Again, go across the hall and see the ivory figures. Note how elongated they are. At the end of the hall you will see an ivory statue of Hodegetria, Mother of God. She must be very important, there's a picture of her in a dictionary. She is holding the Christ child (who looks like a mini-man) who has his hand raised in symbolic greeting. Note the elongated quality and everything else said about this period in the other sheets. Now you may say, "Well, this is all good and well but what period is this anyway?" If you haven't guessed by now, well, this is the Byzantine period.

Now you can leave this hall. Go out and to the right and round the corner. You should be in the Romanesque chapel and you should see a cross facing you. To the left of the cross is a Madonna. Compare it in your mind to the Hodegetria. To the left of the Madonna is a double capital (two columns). Note the gargoyles and stuff. A little further to the front is a column. On the top of this column is a man astride a lion. It represents man overcoming evil. There are also people holding the lion's tail and one of his front paws. Even further up is another column. On top of this one is a centaur which represents man's untamed passions. Now take a good look at the cross and the other things and go straight out of the hall through the medieval section into another section. Do an about-face and look at an incomplete mosaic. This and all the other mosaics that you saw are copies.

Now you may do as you please, at least within the range of the law. (Remember Hunter reputation, girls.) We sincerely hope that you enjoyed this tour. Get back to school on time, and, ah . . . don't take any wooden nickels.

*   *   *   *   *   *

Humanities Museum Tour
The Metropolitan Museum of Art
Fifth Avenue and 82nd Street

This tour was designed in the belief that cultures, civilizations, and empires do not die with the ringing of the 2:10 bell. We hope that art and history will take on a new meaning for you. Spend some time looking and thinking about the pieces you will see on this tour and remember that men and not history books created them.

When you approach the museum, stop to notice the contruction of the front of the building itself. Notice the columns directly in front of the entrance and along the Fifth Avenue side. See if you can recognize their style.

Upon entering the great Hall you can see four sets of columns on each of four sides of the Hall leading to different sections of the Museum. Are they the same as the ones outside?

At this point, get hold of a floor plan at the information desk.
Continue left towards the hall of Greek and Roman art, noticing the columns and the statuary. Continue toward the solitary huge column which stands in front of the restaurant. The columns surrounding the fountain are of a different style. Can you tell what it is?

Now go downstairs to the Ground Floor. You will enter a room which concentrates on Egyptian, Greek and Roman displays. There you should find a model of the Parthenon as it originally stood. Look inside this model to see Athena. In the cases you can see scale models of the Greek city-states of Delphi and Olympia. In Delphi you can see the amphitheater and the Temple of Apollo. Sacred shrines and the Temple of Zeus are in Olympia. Take time to read the museum explanations. The plateau of the Acropolis is represented as it stood in 1895. Contrast the structures in ruins with their original state. Not of relevance but certainly of interest is the reproduction of the Rosetta Stone on the wall (two points from World History)

Virtually all the museums are delighted to have students visit when they come with a specific purpose and ask questions. In several instances a curator can be persuaded to meet with a group of students and explain the operations of the museum. In virtually all instances the museums are pleased to have schools borrow slides prior to their visit. Properly planned, museum visits can prove to be illuminating experiences rather than merely an excuse to leave school.

Schools that deny students opportunities to become familiar with the wonders of museums, art galleries, the theatre, orchestral music, dance and opera are guilty of gross dereliction of duty. The children can be maimed for life. Long after formal schooling has ended, cultural centers serve as an intellectual and aesthetic nourishment for adults. Not to expose students to the educational and emotional adventures of such visits is unpardonable.

Museums provide convenient brochures on what, where, how and why to see their special and regular exhibitions. If a school is more than a commuter's ride away from a cultural center, transportation and other costs should be budgeted in the same manner as funds are allocated to outfit and transport the basketball and football teams. As an absolute minimum, schools can import a museum's readily available slides, films, posters, records, and other aids to understanding via the first or second class mail routes. To plead poverty or distance as the excuse for depriving students of experiences with the arts is unacceptable.

Whenever visits to the arts are planned the emphasis must be on working with, rather than doing to, students. Once the students feel that a museum is theirs to explore, they become involved and interested. When students sense that they are only spectators they come waiting to be entertained. In schools where teachers can both entertain and educate, the problem of student involvement is not a serious concern. "Open their mouths with laughter and slip knowledge inside," is how one staff member describes his process of teaching. Most teachers are neither so gifted nor glib. But nearly all teachers can develop programs whereby the students become partners in the learning process. In terms of how to make learning linger longer as part of each student's inner vocabulary, the involvement method has no peers. Indeed, the one formula that all humanities programs must adopt, if it is hoped students will live what is learned, is their involvement.

CHAPTER 8

Evaluating a
Humanities Curriculum

How can a school system make valid judgments as to the relative degree of success or failure of its humanities curriculum? One episode in the cartoon strip "Peanuts" comes to mind. Lucy protests to Linus, "I have a lot of questions about life and I'm not getting any answers." To which Linus replies, "Would true or false be all right?"[1]

We must do better than true or false, but objective criteria applied to subjective values are hard to substantiate. Here, for example, are four goals a humanities curriculum could consider as direction points on which to base evaluation:

1. A sustained, deliberate attempt to synthesize and relate learning from different disciplines, to the end that the students' learning will be less fragmented and more meaningful.

2. An examination of the ways in which some great human beings have defined for themselves what it means to be a

---

[1] From *PEANUTS* © 1969, United Feature Syndicate, Inc.

human being, to the end that students will search for their own "humanness," too.

3. In individual creative projects, students will draw upon their own interests and abilities to enjoy the satisfactions of work well done, to the end that they further identify and individuate themselves.

4. Through group planning and teaching, the humanities teaching team will learn from one another and respect one another's differences, to the end that they acquire broader academic perspectives, and deeper personal insights.

But how can any objective test provide positive proof of an expansion of vision, a more sensitized understanding of people, a greater sense of self-worth, and a commitment to be a contributing member of the human race? The answer: no examination can accurately, objectively measure sensitive and ethical living. We possess no mean Greenwich time value line which everyone can accept. Several built-in evaluative feed-back procedures however can and should be utilized. Here are some:

1. Teacher-student conferences before, during, and at the conclusion of the humanities curriculum.
2. Student critiques of student work.
3. Questionnaires.
4. The number of students who elect the program each year.
5. Willingness of the administration, the school board, and the community to support the program.

THE STUDENT QUESTIONNAIRE

An evaluative questionnaire devised by the students and the humanities staff will provide some meaningful answers. The following is one example taken by 105 students:

On balance, given your experience to date in the humanities curriculum (April), would you recommend this program to next year's seniors?

95 Yes   2 No

  48 Enthusiastically   0 Strongly negatively

  36 Fairly strongly   2 Fairly negatively

  11 In a lukewarm way   0 Neutral, don't care
                                     either way

8 *No Reply*

On balance, given your experience to date in the humanities curriculum (April), would you say you're glad you elected it?

97 Yes   2 No

  53 Enthusiastically   1 Strongly negatively

  30 Fairly strongly   0 Fairly negatively

  14 In a lukewarm way   1 Neutral, don't care
                                     either way

6 *No reply*

Since the papers were not signed, no grades were involved, and the students both distributed and compiled the results, one can believe that the answers truly reflected honest opinion. Replies to the next question indicate relative levels of interest and success:

Which aspects of the humanities curriculum, if any, have you enjoyed and found worthwhile?

Workshops	93
Large group sessions for art slides	36
Large group sessions for films	77
Large group sessions for faculty or guest lectures	41
Musuem trips	76
Walking tours in and out of city	82
Required cultural events, ballet, opera, etc.	38
Opportunity to read and discuss "great works"	77
Opportunity to write on "great works"	14
Flexibility of scheduling	72
Making frescoes, urns, etc.	62
Talk sessions evaluating program	84
No grades	36

Several of the comments written below each question deserve special mention.

> "This program has brought the class together like nothing else could do. Up to this year we students sat in the same rooms but we never had a chance to really know one another—to discuss our values, our backgrounds, our hopes and frustrations. The whole format made for a different, healthy relationship between student and student and even student and teacher."

> "We learned to listen to one another."

> "Changing teachers each time we changed books—and changing the student composition after each theme—meant we had a no static situation."

> "I learned things about myself in the drama workshop that I never knew before."

> "Last year in English class we read the *Odyssey*. This year in humanities we did the *Iliad*. I enjoyed the *Iliad* much more. Why? Because the English class was cut each day after 40 minutes. In humanities we have more time each day but we do not go on endlessly day after day for an entire month with the same book. There's less dragging in humanities."

Here is an interim evaluation form students could complete after the first quarter of the term:

1. What books, activities, experiences in this first quarter of the humanities curriculum did you like the most? Please explain.
2. What did you like the least? Please explain.
3. What did we do that you wished we did more?
4. What did we neglect that you wish we included?
5. What aspects of the program, if any, would you recommend for consideration by the rest of the school? Why? And *not* recommend? Why?

STRUCTURING FOR HONEST ANSWERS

Even the devil has learned how to lie with statistics. Nonetheless information supplied by the students themselves is as accurate an evaluation gauge as one can develop if several safeguards are built into the questionnaire:

1. anonymity—each student must feel that no person will be able to identify the author—unless the evaluator wished for some personal reason to identify herself.

2. seriousness of purpose—if the approach is a frivolous one, answers will not reflect honest opinions.

3. majority response—unless the overwhelming majority of students reply, the results could be weighted in favor of one side with a special interest in answering questions.

4. the nature of the questions—students and teachers must be given every opportunity to test the questions for reliability and validity. Some questions can be "loaded" to prove any position an evaluator desires.

5. tabulation procedures—questionnaire results must be compiled by a non-partisan committee of students and teachers to make certain that all statistics and quotations are accurately reported.

6. comments—ample space must be provided for students to write comments not necessarily germane to the questions.

7. time—if the questionnaire is distributed as a momentary break between periods, or as an afterthought, students will not be afforded sufficient time to answer intelligently. All evaluation questionnaires should be scheduled within the school day or if distributed for return at a later date, the importance of thinking through each question should be fully emphasized.

THE STUDENT FREEDOM SYNDROME

Of course certain dangers inevitably arise when student evaluations become a prime factor in judging a program's strength and survival. What drummers should the faculty hear when deciding on whether and/or how to shape a humanities curriculum? When we lock students into a school system for twelve or thirteen years strains on both the school and the student are inevitable. No matter how effective and enthusiastic the motivation, not all

students will be interested. Our schools are filled with both
voluntary and involuntary youngsters. Some come eagerly to
learn, many more come because they must. For this latter group it
would be wonderful if society had the equivalent of a school bank
in which to hold the accumulated knowledge until desired.
Students could then come to the school bank when they wished or
when they felt that they needed the educational interest available.
Instead, like animals in the circus, all students are forced to
perform each day no matter what their personal situation. Librar-
ies, museums, and correspondence courses provide some types of
educational reservoirs. But by the time many adolescents are no
longer reluctant to grasp the knowledge, perhaps even wisdom,
that schools offer, they are too much in the economic stranglehold
of tedious tasks to break their job routine patterns for learning.
And since society has devised no acceptable alternatives for formal
schooling, young people are forced to follow the educational
lockstep. Ready or not, willing or not, able or not, to school they
come.

This negative appraisal of student attitude toward school has
been documented over and over again. A National Education
Association investigation in 1970 brought forth the following:

> Most kids go to school because they must. School is something
> alien from the real life of adolescents. Even the politically active
> find their release in electioneering work outside of school. The
> school is only a holding action, a grown-up baby-sitting organiza-
> tion before young people are released to college or jobs or the
> military.[2]

Only when students are made to feel that their decisions have
some binding effect, that student power is real and not a charade,
does a school system seem part of a student's life. Offering
students the opportunity to evaluate what they have experienced,
and acting on the findings, is one of the most effective ways to
demonstrate their importance as human beings and as constructive
school partners.

---

[2]Bernard McKenna and Jane Power, eds., *Student Rights and Responsibilities* (Washington, D.C.: National Education Association Task Force on Student Involvement,
October, 1970).

STUDENT PARTICIPATION AS PARTNERS

Until recently students accepted scholastic servitude as the will of man and God,—or they left school. Teachers were told to try three approaches when dealing with reluctant learners—take them gently by the hand, firmly by the arm, or roughly by the neck. A fourth alternative was also utilized. They were ignored. Today, more and more students will not be taken and they refuse to be ignored. They insist on moving at their own momentum. And they have the law of the land on their side.

The doctrine of *in loco parentis* has been giving way in judicial decisions. In the Supreme Court decision of *Tinker vs. Des Moines School District,* the Court ruled:

> First Amendment rights, applied in light of the special characteristics for the school environment, are available to teachers and students ... It can hardly be argued that either students or teachers shed their constitutional rights to freedom of speech or expression at the schoolhouse gate.[3]

Schools must develop alternative paths for students to take while at the same time maintaining educational quality and legitimacy. We will have to develop different programs going on side by side, from the traditional subject orientation for some to derivatives of encounter type sessions as well as individualized projects and mini-courses for others. Old masters may still be hung on the wall but we need new masters to examine, and even new walls. One of the joys of the humanities curriculum is that it does provide such latitude within a defensible educational framework. And it is structured to facilitate student participation and evaluation.

Student participation and evaluation are essential in a humanities curriculum. They must sense that the program is their creation as well as the teachers'. They must see that student-recommended changes are welcomed. They must assume responsibility for what is successful and unsuccessful. When a humanities curriculum offers many options, when the entire community is used as the school's laboratory, when opportunities are available for creative

---

[3]*Tinker vs. Des Moines Independent Comm. Sch. Dist.,* 393 U.S. 503, 506, February 24, 1969.

experiences, for self-discovery, and for fresh cultural perspectives, the problems of student participation and evaluation become manageable. Neither apathy nor anarchy will prevail. Students should be invited, urged, even cajoled, if necessary, to take an active role in setting goals and procedures for the humanities curriculum. Either by election or volunteering, student representatives in sufficient number should meet regularly with the humanities teaching team. As a class, and as individuals, students can detail their successes and disappointments over the school years. And they can be relied upon to indicate their preferences within a humanities curriculum for a program that makes sense. In addition, a questionnaire to every humanities student will give the faculty a clearer picture of student background, interests, and hopes upon which to structure the curriculum. A questionnaire, if utilized in good faith for scheduling purposes will do much more: when students feel that their "in-put" is considered, they will be more willing to serve as participants and become involved with evaluation. The questionnaires themselves should be designed, distributed, and analyzed by the students as well as the humanities staff. Here is one such questionnaire:

HUMANITIES QUESTIONNAIRE

Name_____

You may answer by writing in checks or single words in the spaces provided, but please feel free to write in any additional information, specific examples wherever you can, or any category which we have left out.

Music

_____ 1. I have had training in_____for_____
             years.

_____ 2. I spend very little time listening to music.

_____ 3. I spend a lot of time listening to music ( )at concerts,
             ( )on radio, ( )on the phonograph or tape recorder,
             ( )performed by me and my friends.

_____ 4. The kinds of music I like are (write in period or style if
             you wish)

             ( )opera   ( )chamber music   ( )symphonies,
             ( )jazz   ( )folk, rock, pop   concerts

_____ 5. My favorite works or performing artists include:

Dance

_____ 1. I have studied_____ for _____years.

_____ 2. I don't go to dance performances.

_____ 3. I like to attend dance events, or watch them on T.V., including ( )ballet, ( )modern dance, ( )ethnic or folk, ( )mixed media performances

_____ 4. I would like to know more about dance forms, such as

_____.

_____ 5. Some favorite works or performers in dance include:

Art

_____ 1. I have had instruction in ( )painting, ( )drawing, ( )sculpture, ( )ceramics, ( )photography, ( )fashion design, ( )lettering

_____ 2. I like to do (any of the above _____) although I have not had formal lessons, and I am pretty good at it.

_____ 3. I think I am hopeless at creating art.

_____ 4. I would like to know how to_____ .

_____ 5. I never go to galleries or museums unless forced to.

_____ 6. I go to museums or galleries often. Some I have liked are:

_____ 7. I have read books on art or artists, such as:

_____ 8. I collect and display some kinds of art in my home:

Artists I especially like include:

Literature

_____ 1. I read works of literature other than those assigned in class, such as: ( )current novels, ( )novels of the past, ( )biographies, ( )poetry, ( )plays, ( )criticism (book reviews)

_____ 2. I never read any literature except that assigned in class

_____ 3. I go to plays (how often _____) including:

_____ 4. I listen to poetry or plays on records, such as:

_____ 5. I like to write ( )poetry, ( )stories, ( )plays

_____ 6. I have been involved in play production as ( )actress, ( )director, ( )technician

_____ 7. I go to movies: frequently? seldom? I especially enjoy these:

_____ 8. I watch television a great deal, and especially like:

_____ 9. Periodicals I regularly read include:

Social Studies

_____ 1. I have read books other than class texts in these areas: ( )philosophy, ( )archeology, ( )anthropology, ( )religion, ( )economics, ( )history, ( )government and politics

_____ 2. I have been active in practical politics, doing_____ _____.

_____ 3. I am not the least bit interested in current politics.

_____ 4. Political leaders or thinkers of the past or present whom I admire include:

Political figures of past or present who interest me include:

General

At this time I expect to major in _____ at college. My thoughts about a life career have included_____ _____.

Some typical student comments reveal the complexities schools must face when seeking to meet their expectations:

"All our lives we have been given knowledge. Now we want to use it, to create on our own. . . . "

"Do not lead us by the hand to the museum or tell us what to see . . . "

"Let us make the decisions on what we read or do in class . . . "

"What I want may not be what I really need and what I like

least may be what I need most. But I will only learn the truth by finding out myself, not by hearing the truth from you . . . "

"We want neither useless freedom nor regimentation . . . "

"Encourage our creative energies and allow for failure . . . Can't we have a school where the idea of failure simply doesn't exist? . . . "

"Give us a chance to explore ourselves for the first and possibly the last time . . . "

"Let us write books. We think we can compete with the adult world on their level . . . "

How difficult it is to provide for both competition and cooperation, to recognize the fine lines between student confidence, student uncertainty, and student arrogance!

Students should be consulted many times before a humanities curriculum is instituted. Should they also meet with the humanities staff throughout the academic year? At Hunter the original plan was to invite student reaction and evaluation at the conclusion of each of the four units. Student comments could then serve as a basis for structural revision of each succeeding theme. No member of the faculty contemplated meeting with a student committee on a weekly basis to discuss and develop future plans when the humanities curriculum was initially conceived.

But the students came with precisely this request. They wished, more, they demanded, to be involved in the humanities curriculum not only as willing participants but as eager, equal formulators of policy. The faculty indicated that to bring students into the teacher planning sessions would eliminate the important element of surprise which each new weekly schedule occasioned. Every week the faculty literally knocked themselves out planning at least one novel experience either inside or outside the school. An architectural tour—("bring your cameras to school tomorrow")—a movie with Hollywood film stars that underscored the current theme *(Lion in Winter, A Man For All Seasons, Henry V,* etc.) guests, film slides, visits, special food desserts, art exhibitions, etc. Students looked forward to receiving the weekly humanities schedule. But if students served on the planning team the element of surprise, of anticipation, would be gone. Without hesitation the students expressed a willingness to sacrifice surprise for the right to meet with the faculty and to plan each week's program in detail.

After some debate the faculty agreed that having student representation on a daily basis to participate and evaluate would be a healthy situation for the humanities curriculum. Whenever problems dealing with individual students were to be discussed, or matters exclusively the concern of teachers, a faculty executive session could be held. Four students from the morning humanities and an equal number from the afternoon program were elected by the students as their representatives. Representation changed with each change of theme although some students were reelected for a second term. Almost never were formal notes taken on any issue; always it was a matter of reaching for consensus. Never did a question arise which placed all the faculty on one side and all the students on the other.

What does a faculty say when it agrees to meet with students as partners? It recognizes that the old forms of legitimacy which decreed that teachers could meet together in cozy corners and determine curricula for students will no longer suffice. Certainly our younger teachers coming to the school house do not accept curriculum control as an inherent right of tenured educators. Neither do parents.

Sharing curricula powers with students does present problems. Who are the representative students? Do they truly reflect the thinking of their peers? Are they representatives or do they voice the concerns of active constituencies with special axes to grind? The answers will be determined by the nature of the school and the procedures used to encourage the election of candidates. A student-teacher community must be held together by a sense of community. They must talk to one another and share some overriding values about scope and direction of the humanities curriculum. When students come to these sessions from separate rather than from consensus constituencies the whole act of give and take, the life blood of a committee, becomes difficult to achieve. As at the United Nations, the delegates are not then free agents who are able to think for themselves. If student representatives come to planning sessions of the humanities staff with hardened positions, little progress can be anticipated. A holding company philosophy will only result in disorder and despair.

—And the same limitation on constructive student-faculty interaction applies to the teachers.

Additional membership on planning sessions means additional voices and additional time needed for meetings. Some student representatives will take on the role of teacher, some will challenge every idea, some are full of ideas, some are virtually worthless. If in a faculty's desire to show good faith and act democratically, no firm guidelines are established for student-teacher discussions, difficulties can be anticipated. Precious time will often be spent or wasted on nonconsequential items. Problems of personalities may become more urgent than programs or procedures. Often the sessions will end on a note of frustration when all that has to be discussed and decided about the specific format of the next week's humanities curriculum is neglected.

At the end of the first year of the Hunter humanities curriculum students complained in their evaluation sessions that the faculty was too democratic. "We are of too many different opinions to formulate policy," they declared. "Listen to us, but the final decision should be yours." Such confidence on the part of the young people toward adults only comes after a crucible of experience. Even then faith in faculty decision-making is of tenuous duration. —And each new class of students will provide a new testing ground before trust is extended. Neither Tevya's children in *Fiddler on the Roof* nor the children in the present generation will accept tradition as reason enough. The young wish to create their own traditions—traditions which in turn will be called rigidities by the next generation.

SENSITIVITY TO YOUTH

One of the striking features of the humanities curriculum is the possibility of breaking down traditional distrust and automatic hostile reponses from students. In most school situations we teach subjects, not students. Even in schools where teacher friendship and informality are hallmarks of conduct, students tend to consider most adults as foreigners. Teachers and administrators do have academic power to restrict student freedom, and they exercise it. And students, as teen-agers, think the majority of the faculty is too old and far too removed from their "real world" to understand the gut concerns of youth. A teacher is flattered when a dozen years after graduation, her student returns to say how young she is. Actually it is the now older student's vision that has changed as to what constitutes a young outlook. We need, while students are still in school, to have each one aware that we regard them as human beings, as persons, as somehow different from other students in the same classroom. In small communities the teacher who lives where she works can know the special problems and joys each child is experiencing outside the school walls. The local newspaper is one handy source. Just shopping in the stores will give insights and recognition. And meeting parents on the street, in church, and at meetings will provide further details with which teachers can relate in a personal way to students in her classes. Larger communities make such contacts more difficult. More reliance must be placed on the guidance counselor who should seek out and make available the personal data teachers need. But even in metropolitan areas teachers can be interested in where a student went over the weekend, what they did last summer, what programs they watch, whether they have any favorite teams, whether they work after school,—the human questions which make all the difference in the world in developing solid student-teacher bonds.

Antoine De Saint-Exupery grasped this dimension of distance in adults in his beautiful book *The Little Prince:*

> Grown-ups love figures. When you tell them that you have made a new friend, they never ask you any questions about essential matters. They never say to you, "What does his voice sound like? What games does he love best? Does he collect butterflies?" Instead, they demand: "How old is he? How many brothers has he? How much does he weigh? How much money does his father make?" Only from these figures do they think they have learned anything about him ... they are like that. One must not hold it against them. Children should always show great forbearance toward grown-up people.[4]

---

[4]Antoine De Saint-Exupery, *The Little Prince* (New York: Harcourt, Brace and World, Inc., New York, 1943), pp. 17-18.

Even the most sensitized humanities teaching teams can fail to judge student feelings. One example: in the second year of the humanities curriculum at Hunter the faculty wished to combine both morning and afternoon groups for a joint venture dealing with the current theme—the Greeks. When a humanities curriculum includes two separate groups of students in morning and afternoon sessions, it is advisable for both groups to be united from time to time in order to exchange ideas, to provide variety, and to share experiences that cannot be readily duplicated. In the main a school faculty will recognize this need and will not object to an occasional joint excursion even though their students would thereby be absent from either morning or afternoon classes. Needless to say faculty and administration should know of such plans long before they are scheduled.

At a meeting of the humanities faculty, the decision was made to take the students to Yale University. By hiring several buses and traveling to this exciting college away from New York we hoped to provide a social as well as intellectual atmosphere for all the students. One of the humanities teachers was a John Hay Fellow who had spent her Fellowship year at Yale University. "Yale University abounds with Greek motifs," she stated. "We can take an architectural tour of the university and contrast Greek buildings with their modern counterparts." When she discovered that Professor Scully, one of Yale's great teacher-scholars, would allow our students to attend a lecture on Greek architecture which he had scheduled for undergraduates on the same day as our proposed trip, all of us were overjoyed with anticipation. So certain were we of our decision that no teacher even bothered to consider whether the students would be equally excited.

When the students were informed of our plans, they reacted coldly. "Why weren't we consulted before final arrangements were made? Why commit us to spend $2.00 for a bus ride without asking if we wish to go?" were some of the questions thrown at the faculty. Of course, some students were delighted with the idea and after the day was spent at Yale, virtually all the humanities students expressed satisfaction in having gone. (In the next issue of the school newspaper, the seniors not in the humanities program protested that the humanities staff was discriminatory for not including them in the Yale trip!) The reaction to our

introduction of the Yale University experience served as a sober
reminder that students wish to be involved in every phase of the
humanities curriculum which concerns them. Later in the year
when the faculty hit on the idea of a week-long film festival as a
break and bridge between units, student opinion was actively
solicited and students participated in film selections. All people,
young and not so young, seem to enjoy most and remember
longest, what they do themselves.

TO GRADE OR NOT TO GRADE

"Are you going to grade us on all this?" and "Do we have to
know all this for the test?" are the most discouraging, the most
devastating questions students can ask. The questions reveal much
about the nature of our schools. "All this" means that the level of
understanding will be surface deep, retained just long enough to
regurgitate on the examination. "All this" means no matter how
important the concept, how related to the past, how necessary for
the future, little residue will remain.

Why are such questions heard so often in our schools? Primarily
because students have been conditioned to respond in this fashion.
A student would explain:

> The teacher holds us responsible for certain information. In order
> to have a minimum of trouble in school we need to fill the
> teacher's prescription—to memorize what she thinks is important
> for us to know on a test. Since what goes on in school has little
> effect on my out-of-school life, I do in school what the school
> people require—and little else.

And teachers use grades as a weapon, as a means to force
compliance; worst of all, as an end in itself. We need grades for
the report card, for the record office, for college, for the
employment agency and the state education department. That
grades should serve as an evaluation of teacher as well as pupil,
that grades should be the basis for reteaching and relearning rather
than as a threat, is rarely considered. (In at least one school final
examinations are given more than a month before the end of the
school year. In this way students and teachers can review material
and concepts that are not fully understood). Nor can teachers be
sanguine about the reliability of their grading practices. Certainly

teacher subjectivity in determining credits for essay answers is an ancient scandal. And the questionable validity of objective type tests raises serious doubts whether the grading system deserves to be considered untouchable.

ELIMINATING GRADES

In theory, when students are given the opportunity to study what they see as purposeful, grades become meaningless. Students will then learn willingly and will not need the grade whip. So the theory goes. Removing grades does demonstrate faculty goodwill and good faith and often students react accordingly. When grades are part of the way of school life students can be expected to ask "What do you want?" on a written assignment. When grades are no longer a consideration students gradually learn to write what they feel is important. Soon the students start asking themselves, "What do I want to say on this topic?"

Instead of grades, a humanities staff can submit an anecdotal report of what each student actually accomplished in seminar sessions and project workshops. Copies of the anecdotal reports should be made available to the student as well as attached to college applications and employment reference forms. On the report card next to the subject "Humanities" can appear the letter "P" for pass. Students who do not seem to profit from their experiences in the humanities curriculum would be withdrawn from the program and no grade or mark noted.

Colleges reacted favorably to the anecdotal report as an evaluative instrument. The following samples of such anecdotal records indicate the range of comments that could be written individually or collectively by a humanities staff:

"Caroline is one of the hardest workers in the Drama Workshop. She had dedicated herself to becoming a professional actress, to the extent of summer stock work and wide play reading. Nothing is too hard; nothing is too small. She designed all the make-up materials, and made up all the students on the day of the workshop performance. Although she is not a brilliant actress, her help and spirit have been invaluable to me. Her eventual field may lie possibly in directing rather than acting because she has made some excellent suggestions which greatly improved my own direction of two scenes. Her absence would leave a big hole in the Drama Workshop.

"Caroline's Seminar work is equally thoughtful. She writes good papers, is conscientious in her reading assignments, and when she learns more tolerance for viewpoints different from her own, she will be an outstanding seminar student."

"Jeanne has been a fine participant in the Cultural Anthropology Workshop. Her comments have been sensible, realistic, perceptive about people and demonstrative of great appreciation of others. In Seminars her interest in literature is clearly evident. Her papers have been good, and in one instance, outstanding. She is enjoying the curriculum and contributing to its success."

"Judy was a member of the City Politics Workshop and her presence generally assured the success of any discussion. She responded to the Yale trip, which she did not wish to take, with a kind of openness to new experience rather rare in students with preconceived ideas. Her honesty in analyzing her own prejudices and why Yale blew them away was pure joy to listen to. Although she still writes rather weak papers, I think Judy has profited from this program to the utmost of her potential."

THE FALLOUT FROM GRADELESSNESS

Until January, when college applications are completed, the vast majority of students in the humanities program will give serious attention to their seminar studies and special projects. After January, the concept of working for one's own self fares less well. Why? A humanities faculty can ask just so much of human nature. Only the most dedicated or the most pliable students are prepared to read, write, and continue intensive research projects on their own when other demands or interests become more pressing. Learning for self-enjoyment in the humanities curriculum is difficult to sustain, for example, when in other elective classes, teachers make demands in the form of tests, grades, papers and deadlines.

Self-learning does not spring forth overnight like Minerva out of Jupiter's head. For as long as they have gone to school students have been taught, carefully taught, to do what they were told, not what they would wish. This well-worn path to success cannot be summarily changed. As with the slaves in Plato's cave, it seems more natural and easier to prefer the darkness to the light.

In the United States external competition has a far higher priority than internal motivation. Virtually all the efforts of school and society concentrate on moving men from without. Car rental agencies, debate teams, and government policy all aim to beat someone, to try harder, to be number one. Young people who wish to do "their own thing" are expressing a response to and a rejection of the competitive world. And schools need to provide more opportunities for learning and doing in order to be self-generating rather than external pump-primers.

A humanities staff should have some basic agreements on what to expect, and what not to tolerate; what minimums of work are necessary to profit from the program, and what standards to set. Hunter's staff, in its first year, had no such agreements. Some wished to remove recalcitrant students, others felt it was wrong to demand that all students conform to any minimum requirements. "We are experimenting. Let us give the students more time to work out their problems themselves. Perhaps our assignments are out of line when a student does not see it as being meaningful to her." Such were some of the points raised by several of the faculty. Due to our indecision, and the constant hope for positive change in student attitude, no student was dropped from the humanities program. The humanities faculty out of kindness, hope and uncertainty, allowed some students to coast along rather than apply themselves.

In the project reports, for example, some teachers set strict limits on what was expected, what time to meet, etc., and in general, the students responded. Other teachers were more permissive in establishing regulations and guidelines and in general, the students responded less well. It can be argued that projects completed under compulsion are not really meaningful. In *The Mikado* the punishment was made to fit the crime; in school the form of regulation should fit the student. Some students require compulsion, order, standards, deadlines. Some thrive as free spirits.

Schools must recognize and make allowances for extremes without jeopardizing the way students who comprise the central core work best.

Students study with different levels of willingness. Desire, fear, respect, tradition, parental expectations, teacher inspiration, and the student's own health, insights, and anticipations play a role in determining school performance. How to keep a balance between freedom and responsibility when a nongraded humanities curriculum is introduced only at the twelfth grade level is no easy assignment. A strong case can be made for exposure to a more open school atmosphere long before the senior year. Begin it must. If the school makes little effort to give students a taste of free choice during their secondary education, the chances are small that they will be ready to cope with a sudden rush of freedom as college freshmen or as adults. To be mistrusted in June as high school seniors and to be trusted in September as undergraduates, laborers and secretaries, makes no sense at all. But if too much restraint is bad, it does not follow that no restraint at all is necessarily better for every student.

After eleven years of schooling, and a much longer period of tenure in the home and society, most students are programmed for rewards. The inner satisfactions gained when accomplishing some significant task, when expanding one's range of knowledge or awareness for his own sake, seem not to be enough. A humanities faculty errs when it assumes that by offering freedom from grades the motivations of students can be changed overnight. Moving from grades to gradelessness, like moving from gravity to weightlessness, requires considerable preparation.

Certainly the use of grades in school and college as a weapon and as a threat requires radical reappraisal. Marks have become another example of the tail wagging the dog. With grades on report cards being the primary way of providing visible evidence of accomplishment, the whole school system, from the students' vantage point, is to work for marks. Placing a grade priority on education encourages and sometimes forces cheating to become the solution as well as the means. Lack of alternate ways to judge worth leads too many to play the grade game, legally if they can, illegally if they must.

Removing grades on a wholesale basis will clear the air of old value patterns. But most human beings are not organized to substitute internal for external rewards once the standardized grade pressures are discarded. Some tokens of praise, some tangible symbols of accomplishment seem necessary for people in capitalistic, communistic, and in primitive orders. Preciously few human beings will be content or self-motivated with the knowledge that the reward is entirely personal, entirely unknown to others. Thus the simplistic solution of removing grades is no solution at all. Unless alternative systems of rewards are established, most students will flounder. Man's inner strength, goodwill, and desire to be creative cannot stand alone. Legal and social imperatives must undergird in some visible way the positive impulses of humanity. If we should not say about man, as did Pavlov, "How like a dog," neither, alas, can we say with Shakespeare, "How like an angel." Our schools and our society should devise reward systems that develop the positive, cooperative possibilities in young people. The present grading system offers too narrow a prism.

SUBSTITUTES FOR GRADES

Teachers sensitized to the human qualities of youth have always utilized grade substitutes. The boy who works to the level of his ability deserves to be commended for his efforts. If the report card grade cannot indicate such effort, a teacher can. A word of praise in class, a remark outside the classroom, a note on his paper, a letter to his parents, a recommendation report to the guidance counselor, a request that he show others his procedure, a special invitation to a club meeting,—these are only a few methods teachers have available to recognize individuality. Doing away with the rank-in-class loadstone will help students be more concerned with the search in research than with the grades. So will more courses that students can audit, and courses where only the letter grades "P" or "F" are used. In several schools where student accomplishment is evaluated with anecdotal records rather than grades, the report card will be limited to the single designation "P" or "CR", meaning credit received. Students who do not wish to work are asked to withdraw from the program and take the traditional regular courses instead.

Essential to the success of substituting other rewards for grades is an explanation of the reasons for the new policy. Students should be informed at the very first session of the school year what is expected, what trust is placed in them, why certain books, etc., were chosen, why grades have been eliminated, and the consequences of non-cooperation. We discovered for example that only about half the students had read the two books assigned for summer study, Homer's *Iliad* and Camus' *The Plague*. Some students had borrowed editions of the *Iliad*. They found the writing style too stilted and stuffy and so they abandoned Homer. Many students were too fully occupied with summer sun, spirit, and sightseeing to take time out for reading. The teaching staff indicated in no uncertain terms, after students demonstrated a paucity of knowledge in the seminar sessions, that to continue the seminars would be a waste of time. "Our humanities curriculum is deliberately structured as a loose-boned program with no grades. It is designed for students who wish to learn and share. Each student's contributions to the seminar discussions are expected and welcomed. If you have no desire or ability to do the reading and sharing we ask you to leave and enter classes where formal grades will keep you active." The message was received. While the level of student participation continued to vary at times from exuberant to lackluster, the overall commitment of students to the concept of sharing ideas was both solid and substantial.

Students need to feel free to express themselves, to explore, to make mistakes. They need limits, too,—limits that encompass the golden rule, limits they understand and accept even though everyone cannot agree in all particulars. Students, teachers, and school administrators—all must be aware of boundary lines that safeguard their individualities as well as the individuality of others. Within this broad framework a school can provide the freedom for a viable humanities curriculum.

"It is the first step of . . . wisdom," Alfred North Whitehead said, "to recognize that the major advances in civilization are processes which all but wreck the societies in which they occur . . . The art of free society consists first in the maintenance of the symbolic code; and secondly in fearlessness of revision . . . Those societies which cannot combine reverence to their symbols with freedom of revision, must ultimately decay . . . "[5] Some system of rewards is inherent in our symbolic code; a humanistic curriculum offers the "fearlessness of revision" to keep schools relevant within a broad boundary line that provides continuity between yesterday, today and tomorrow.

THE MORAL ARISTOCRACY

How, then, can a humanities curriculum be evaluated in finite terms? I submit that a precise, analytical barometer based solely on how the mind has grown would be an injustice. Humanities' goals deal with a student's growth in style, in tone, in sensitivity as well as in knowledge. As human beings our minds may be our greatest asset but there are some areas where only the heart can command.

A humanities curriculum could be judged successful if the students—and the teachers— have grown to join what E. M. Forster has called the moral aristocracy.

> Not an aristocracy of power, based on rank and influence, but an aristocracy of the sensitive, the considerate, and the plucky . . .
> They are sensitive for others as well as themselves, they are considerate without being fussy, their pluck is not swankiness but the power to endure, and they can take a joke.[6]

Any evaluation must free the mind to act and react, but provision must also be made for the heart to measure and respond. Such a partnership evaluation principle may seem like an impossible assignment for educators. It is—until we consider the alternatives.

Above all, a school's leadership must not impose answers from above. Direct student and teacher involvement is an absolute necessity. If people have to make a choice they will vote for the mistakes of enthusiasm rather than the indifference of wisdom.

---

[5] Alfred North Whitehead, *Symbolism, Its Meaning and Effect* (New York: The Macmillan Company, 1927), p. 88.

[6] E.M. Forster, *Two Cheers for Democracy* (New York: Harcourt, Brace and World, Inc., 1951), p. 73.

We most urgently need a humanistic attitude in our schools; we most urgently need a humanities curriculum because it offers participatory options instead of submission. The humanities can restore what is fast becoming lost in modern life—an environment in which reverence for learning is based on individual choice and understanding, as well as on mutual commitment. Schools that seek to be humanistically oriented will integrate education and life. I can conceive of no more urgent goal for students who are currently making decisions about themselves—and will be making decisions on local, national and world issues before 1984, and beyond.

Index